THE GOD

WHO SHOWS

HIMSELF

Carl F. H. Henry

THE GOD
WHO SHOWS
HIMSELF

By Carl F. H. Henry

WORD BOOKS • WACO • TEXAS

FOREWORD

The appearance of these lectures and addresses in book form recalls many pleasant platform and pulpit associations of recent months, and creates an opportunity to express public appreciation for the warm welcome of these diverse audiences.

Most of these messages have been delivered to several gatherings, although initially prepared for a specific audience. But at the prompting of Evangelist Billy Graham's aide, Dr. Stan Mooneyham, they are here collected under a single title for wider reading. I trust that the volume will not disappoint this expectation of Christian interest.

The second, third, fifth and last addresses were given at Dallas Theological Seminary as the 1965 Griffith Thomas Memorial Lectures. This I considered a special privilege, since I owe a personal debt reaching back to student days to the edifying writings of that gifted Anglican evangelical scholar of the past generation. Two of these essays have appeared in *Bibliotheca Sacra,* and are reprinted by permission. The fifth lecture was also given at a Wake Forest University student retreat, and provided the occasion of vigorous dialogue and debate with both modernist and neo-orthodox participants.

This present volume takes its title from the first address, which was originally given as one of a series of Tharp Lectures at New Orleans Baptist Theological Seminary. The second address was given also at luncheons of Protestant Men of the Chapel at the U. S. Army War College in Carlisle, Pennsylvania, and at the U. S. Continental Army Command at Fort Monroe, Virginia. The remarks on contemporary involvement summarize an address to a convention of the American Association of Evangelical Students at Bethel College, St. Paul. Later I was asked to repeat this material to a Washington seminar sponsored by the National Association of Evangelicals.

The sixth address was prepared under the original title "Thine is the Kingdom" for the men's convention of the Reformed Church in America in the Grand Rapids civic auditorium.

The essay on "Evangelicals in the Social Struggle" is the only one that has appeared in the pages of *Christianity Today* and it is reprinted here because many readers expressed a desire for its issuance in more permanent form.

The address on education and religion was given at Taylor University in Indiana during inaugural week ceremonies attending the installation of Dr. Milo A. Rediger as president and the same weekend to the seventh annual Christian American Heritage Seminar on the John Brown University campus in Arkansas. The remarks on ecumenism were initially presented on an assigned subject as part of a religious emphasis series at Wayne State University, Detroit. As the reader can easily imagine, the meeting erupted into explosive public dialogue with local ecumenical enthusiasts.

As editor of *Christianity Today,* frequent invitations have come my way to address American audiences. But the pressure of meeting deadlines has dictated more declinations than acceptances. Perhaps some groups will give me this further hearing through the printed page. The fact that we have often met this way before, in the pages of *Christianity Today,* nourishes my hope that they will consider the encounter worthwhile. Here, as there, I have tried to point the way to a profounder evangelical impact on the contemporary scene.

Carl F. H. Henry

Arlington, Virginia

CONTENTS

Chapter I

THE GOD WHO SHOWS HIMSELF

The Christian concept of God is no mere literary portrait or even pious fiction. Were Christianity's impact on these times simply a matter of cleverness and cuteness, it could hardly allay the spiritual and cultural hungers of modern life. To recall Rabbi Sandmel's observation on contemporary theology, the message more than its manner of expression determines theology's lasting power and lasting satisfaction. Unlike many modern movements skilled in communication and propaganda, Christianity does not rely upon verbal and literary manipulation. The Apostle Paul confronts the Corinthians "not with excellency of speech or of wisdom, declaring the testimony of God," but with unwavering determination to "preach Jesus Christ, and him crucified." Only the religion of the true and living God can meet the prime test of theology. Only the God of Biblical theism can provide a theology of substance, relevancy, and durability.

I.

The Biblical revelation of God is especially germane to man's flight to irrationalism. The doctrine of a rational God and His rational creation and revelation boldly confronts the modern revolt against reason. In his series in the London *Observer* on "The Seven Deadly Sins," Christopher Sykes pointedly noted: "The weakness of this new school of no-humanism, no-morality, no-reason, no-art, is surely that its argument depends on an appeal to those moral values which it rejects, notably the love of truth. If I am not mistaken, its followers are in the same philosophical jam as plagues the behaviourists, of whom Aldous Huxley remarked that if their belief in behaviourism is sound, then there is no reason to attach importance to anything a behaviourist may say." Human beings cannot escape the presupposition that truth exists. Wherever they take this presupposition seriously, and seek the whole truth, they must contend with the truth of God and the God of truth.

I remember accidentally jostling another hurrying traveler at a snack bar in Grand Central Station. Noting his liturgical garb, I asked: "Sir, what one fact makes the Christian view of God especially relevant to man in the modern culture crisis?" He asked me to repeat the question. Then he replied: "The Judeo-Christian doctrine of God is man's only intelligent hope in this present world where he must live out whatever life he is given, and is also the only consistent hope for life in the world to come." While his answer was incomplete, it was good as far as it went. The Christian revelation of God fully satisfies the minds of men; it is consistent with itself and with all that we are and know. This great fact reinforces its validity at a time when speculative solutions often lead mankind to the brink of anti-intellectualism and despair.

But the relevance of the Christian doctrine of God does not stop here. For the very reason that Christianity addresses all life and experience, it touches man's other dilemmas. With substantial relevance Christianity penetrates every major problem of our day.

II.

Amid the much-publicized summit meetings of world leaders, in the "cult of personality" rivalries of our time, and among the "names that make the news," God seems often the only "no show"—to borrow a familiar phrase in modern travel. Actually, of course, one great and unique fact about the Christian view is that God indeed does "show Himself." I recall lunching with a leading Wall Street financial analyst when a minister in the party— very much to the point—emphasized that by thrusting Himself into history the Christian God unmistakably manifests His presence.

From the secular human perspective, today's upheavals often seem erratic and meaningless. One day Cuba is in turmoil, the next, Laos; then Berlin; then Indonesia; then Congo. Action and reaction rumble around the world. These events disclose a certain connection, of course, when comprehended through such strategic literature as Marx's *Communist Manifesto,* Hitler's *Mein Kampf,* Khrushchev's five-year-plan, and so on. Not until the events of each decade have actually become historical record, however, can we confidently decide which of the contemporary plans is really in control. Even then, how can we be sure that the same pattern will continue into even the immediate future?

Not subject to such uncertainties, however, is another corpus of strategic literature which relates these smaller crises of each passing generation within the larger crisis of history. To discerning readers it brings the sure conviction that it is God who shows Himself at the true summits of history; that it is His name above all others that really makes the news.

That God reveals Himself in history means supremely that

Jesus Christ as the God-man is the unveiled deity. He lived a perfect life in the flesh and under our conditions; He bore our imperfections that we might have eternal life. In this manifested Lord the personalities not only of the present but of all time more than meet their match. In Jesus Christ fallen man meets his maker and his remaker, his arbiter or his judge.

What Christian theology means by the Word becoming flesh is radically unique. God's self-disclosure in Christ is the supreme attestation of the Biblical doctrines of divine transcendence and divine incarnation. In the Old Testament God manifests His glory by towering far above the creature and the creation; "graven images" are forbidden, for the confining time-space limits of such material representations conceal infinity and spirituality. In the New Testament God shows His glory in the incarnation, in the fact of "God with us" in Jesus Christ.

Recent existential attempts to protect divine transcendence by emphasizing God's "wholly otherness" undermine divine incarnation and cancel intelligible revelation. In the existential encounter the God who supposedly "shows" never intrudes into history long enough to leave a calling card. But in the Gospels God appears in the incarnate, crucified and risen Christ, and thus divinely and decisively confronts man in regard to life's purpose and that of society. The God who is other than the whole creation steps into history; in Jesus Christ He becomes blood-brother to those adopted into the family of faith. In showing Himself, the God of Biblical theism inscribes His character and purpose not only upon the world of nature and in the conscience of man, but also in the Scriptures. Through the inspired word of the holy prophets and apostles the self-revealing God prepared the way for the incarnate Word of the holy Son. This sacred record of salvation history presents a comprehensive clue to universal history—its point of beginning, its critical mid-point, and its end-point. It affirms, too, divine control of decisive events in the story of mankind. God is pre-eminently the God who in showing Himself shows us up for what we are.

Is God a "no show" in the affairs of our own century? Have such remarkable developments as the political movements toward world government and the return of the exiled Jews to the land of Palestine no intimation in Scripture? The resurgence of ancient powers like Egypt and Syria and Israel to participate in the modern dialogue of nations has bizarre end-time aspects. If Jesus Christ gives the summons to a final judgment of the nations, is it likely that a Soviet veto will delay their assembly or that Christ will default? Is not Jesus Christ to return in power and great glory to cap the course of human events? Will He be a "no show"?

To develop the doctrine of God in Biblical terms is therefore to speak inevitably of Jesus Christ, and to speak of Him not simply by way of preface but by way of climax. It is the false gods who never "show," whose material existence is simply the temporary reality of plastic idols, and whose life ultimately is a matter of but literary fiction or pious imagination. The God of the Bible—of creation, redemption and judgment—is the true God who towers above all others but who shows His face and bares His heart in Jesus Christ. In disclosing Himself He discloses our miserable plight. Revealing our human comedy as part of an eternal drama, He plays havoc with our pageantry, and makes a spectacle of our spectaculars.

In Biblical Christianity, Christology is not merely an ideology for a program of social ethics as it was for Protestant liberalism. *Christianity is Christ!* This declaration gives speculative theologians no license for metaphysical agnosticism, no justification to emphasize only historical and experiential as over against eternal factors in the nature of God. Just the contrary. The truth about God's Son— His incarnation, His cross, His resurrection, His ascension, His return—is truth also about very God of very God. Without this truth, knowledge about God is truncated and even distorted, and misses the full height and depth of God's stature. Jesus Christ is no mere divine envoy; He is the foundation and object of Christian faith because He is God Himself manifest in the flesh.

Sometimes Jesus Christ is rejected as the revelation of God's very nature for such artificial "reasons" as the preservation of "monotheism," the "purity" of Judaism, the teaching of the Koran, the intimations of "natural theology," the "universal witness of God," "existential encounter," and so on. Such rejection of the centrality of Jesus Christ, however, soon mounts a Trojan horse that escorts an enemy-theology into the city of faith to exchange the Living God for a lie. This alien theology may here and there find residual points of contact with certain details of the scriptural accounts. But by evading the unique validity of Jesus Christ as the supreme disclosure of deity it soon aligns itself with some new and false god.

Jesus Christ is both God's First Word (John 1:1) and God's Last Word (John 1:18, Hebrews 1:3). "He that hath seen me hath seen the Father" (John 14:9). Any exposition of theology not centered in the flesh and blood reality of the incarnation is therefore no Biblical theology. The glory of the Christian religion is its worship of the God who "shows."

III.

The Biblical revelation of God therefore uncovers many hidden aspects of the current malaise. Prominent among our quandaries is the modern quest for peace, a search which seems constantly thwarted by the continuous struggle between power and justice. Inability of nations to moralize their might, and incapacity of statesmen to balance war and peace on the scales of justice, come into proper focus through the penetrating light of the Christian docrine of God.

The doctrine of the sovereignty of the holy God exemplifies the absolute morality of power. It exhibits omnipotence in the service of righteousness and righteousness in the service of omnipotence. Emphasis on the kingly office of Christ was never more needful than now. For once God's righteous sovereignty becomes obscure, fallen man becomes skeptical that power can be morally employed. The political actualities of history seem to substantiate this doubt. When might and righteousness are no longer compatibly related, a sinful society either succumbs to the ambitions of power or lacks strength and muscle to defend justice. Strong nations exploit power for unjust ends; weak nations consider every use of power to be corrupt; and pacifists decry war as the worst of all possible evils. If statesmen tend to trust in power irrespective of justice, then the citizenry will certainly become cynical of power, or will rely likewise on power independently of morality.

To efface the principle of divine sovereignty, moreover, promotes the illusion of state sovereignty, or the myth that the United Nations simply by its own decree can permanently fix national boundaries. These moods betray a distrust either of the morality of power or of the power of morality. That is, they discount whatever elements of virtue are reinforced by confidence in God's sovereignty.

Whenever a live sense of the divine morality of power is suppressed, sovereign states are encouraged to seek their ends through the amoral use of power. Or they depend on

morality apart from supportive external strength, on verbal
proclamations which would subject power to the service
of justice but which lack the will to act consistently and
courageously on this conviction.

Even a hasty look at almost any hymn book discloses
how Christians through the centuries have prized "prevailing power," "unfailing power," "transforming power" in
the context of the character of divinity. Without this knowledge of the holy Lord, modern man can only be chilled
rather than cheered by such reminders of omnipotence. Yet
the omnipotent power of the righteous God is one of the
great themes in the epistle to the Roman Christians, whereby
the Apostle Paul reinforced the faith of believers situated
at the very heart of the world empire of that day. Rome's
military genius had long subjugated one nation after another. Even in Corinth where Paul wrote his letter he
could see the Roman devastation of the glory that once
crowned Greece.

What does the apostle say in his epistle to the Romans?
He points to the power of the Creator in creation. Indeed,
he declares that since the creation of the world the invisible
perfections of God "are clearly seen, being understood by
the things that are made, even his eternal power and Godhead" (1:20). Moreover, what boast had the Romans as
a world power? "For when the one man Abraham was a
hundred years old, and despite the deadness of Sarah's
womb" (3:19) the all-powerful Creator, "who quickeneth
the dead, and calleth those things which be not as though
they were" (3:17) made him "a father of many nations".
Could Rome as a nation glory in any inherent power? It
was God who raised up the Egyptian Pharaohs; when they
held world power it was He who thrust them down again:
"For the scripture saith unto Pharaoh, Even for this same
purpose have I raised thee up, that I might show my power

in thee, and that my name might be declared throughout all the earth" (9:17).

Even more succinctly Paul underscores the answerability of world powers to the sovereign Lord of history: "The powers that be are ordained of God" as agents for human good (13:1, 4). God the omnipotent Minister of Justice holds the nations in His hands. As on Mars Hill Paul had told the Greeks that the Divine Creator establishes the boundaries of the nations (Acts 17:26), so now he reminds the Christians at Rome that the Lord of history also establishes the duty of the nations. The state has no liberty to make itself god (as did the Roman Caesars), nor to attribute its fortunes and calamities to pagan myths (as did the Roman poets). The Living God in no sense owes His existence and vitality to the state; rather, government owes its origin and mission to the Living God.

The power of the righteous Lord, moreover, not only can dull the tyrant's sword, but can smite such foes as sin and death and Satan. When through Adam "death reigned" over all mankind, the sovereign Redeemer-God triumphed over sin and death so "grace might reign through righteousness unto eternal life by Jesus Christ our Lord" (5:21). Though empires crumble about him, what has the believer to fear then if his destinies are latched to the Eternal Conqueror? "Who shall separate us from the love of Christ? Shall tribulation, or distress, or persecution, or nakedness, or peril, or sword? [Shall Communist barbarianism? nuclear warheads? or atomic radiation? The apostle might indeed update the contingencies, but his sure conclusion would remain unchanged.] Nay in all these things we are more than conquerors through him that loved us" (8:35, 37).

Recovery of God's sovereignty would furnish our generation once again with the only reliable constant in inter-

national relations, namely, the will of the holy Lord. Moreover, this holy will would bear as remarkably upon our
scientific probing of other worlds as upon the mounting
perplexities of this sphere. What man believes about the
moral governance of the world inescapably conditions his
day-to-day outlook. To think of life as a lottery and of
human survival as a gamble inevitably dissolves the assurance that "God works all things together for good to them
that love him, to them that are the called according to his
purpose" (Romans 8:28). The man whose only security is
in radar warning systems obviously knows nothing of the
Christian's confidence that "none can pluck" him "out of
Christ's hand," that the unseen Holy Spirit watches over
all life's contingencies.

A recovered vision of righteous power would overarch
the staggering scientific penetration of outer space with a
sense of an operative divine providence. The Creator is not
overawed, let alone terrified, by the inherent power potential
in His creation. But strangely enough, as modern scientific
inquiry advances man's knowledge and control of the
cosmos, his environment confronts him with ever larger
fears of the unknown and unpredictable. The prospect of
scientists at California or Massachusetts Institute of Tech-
nology hovering in a fallout hut to avoid scientific destruction poignantly pictures the creature's tragic search to domi-
nate nature without personal subjection to the Creator.

At a time when fissionable materials, now measured in
megatons of nuclear energy, may well become the single
all-purpose scource of power, man scrutinizes the sidereal
universe with none of the Psalmist's irrepressible conviction:
"The heavens declare the glory of God, and the firmament
showeth his handywork" (Psalm 19:1). Instead, today's
scientist declares his intentions of mounting a space weapons
platform, or of outracing his rivals to the moon. Unlike the

Psalmist he finds no "refuge and strength" in the all-powerful Creator, and readies a backyard shelter against the inevitable fallout of power that rages apart from the control and service of righteousness.

Respect for power above principle soon propels any society to the brink of calamity. When influence is valued more highly than integrity, compulsion more than conviction, and might more than right, the collapse of civilization and culture is always imminent. Any generation that downgrades the importance of uprightness, and that readily trades virtue and honor for authority and rule, soon honors brute force as the secret of worldly success. To suggest that probity and prudence are powerless, that integrity is impotent, or to imply that ethical concerns may jeopardize one's otherwise invulnerable and impregnable status, encourages open bestiality among the multitudes stunned and staggered by man's present failure to moralize power. Already too many persons believe that "muscle, and brawn and beef" go farther in this world than a good conscience and an upright heart. The man who leads with his chin often considers himself more important than the man who loves his neighbor. Our world seems to harbor and to absorb czars, Kaisers, duces, führers—all the modern Pharaohs—with greater ease than it does the messengers of good will, justice, and peace. This tendency marks a reversion from the message of Christ to the mentality of the Caesars.

The God of the Bible is the revelation of omnipotent righteousness and of moral supremacy. He gives the lie to modern notions that injustice is strength, that rectitude is weakness. Because it is righteousness that exalts a nation, injustice and iniquity and all the unregenerate powers of this world must inevitably topple. Death and judgment may and will stamp their unbroken curse on the reign of despots. But no one has ever dared reseal the tomb of Christ. In the familiar Apostles' Creed, Pontius Pilate is now but the object of a preposition in a clause whose subject is Jesus Christ our Lord. The God who empowers the muscle of morality and shines the power of purity is the God who "shows" Himself. Sovereign is the God of truth and virtue. Righteous is Christ Jesus the Lord. And divine empowerment is the work of the Holy Spirit. These truths are intrinsic to the Christian doctrine of God; what they imply for a world unable and unwilling to moralize power is obvious enough. In Biblical theology Satan is a doomed creature. For his forces and minions now abroad in the world the outlook is no less devastating.

IV.

The Christian revelation of God bears not only on the role of reason and power in contemporary life, but also on the place of love.

Today's world is a showplace of murder, assault, robbery, and other crimes against individuals. Even more treacherous culturally, however, is the subtle social justification of mob violence, class warfare, and military aggression. The whole temper of political revolution in our time degrades and debunks the significance of love. Through fake propaganda, a controlled press, false witnesses, secret police, "show trials," and so on, mongers in terror and hate advance "the big lie." The modern tendency makes hate itself a virtue, indeed, repudiates love in its Biblical sense and promotes instead the service of hate. This forthright rejection of love is what bears fearful social significance.

Strong love is impossible without also strong hate. Not to hate evil, therefore, means being a traitor to God and to virtue. It must be indicated, however, that Christianity's context of hate is never ultimately anti-anyone or anything. Whatever hate the Christian religion sanctions simply reflects love for God and man, and consequent disapproval of whatever refuses to be pro-God and pro-neighbor. That man is "a liar" when he professes to love God on the one hand while he hates his brother on the other (I John 4:20) is therefore strikingly relevant to the current social crisis. Hatred, or actual murder of one's brother (I John 3:12), is the only New Testament alternative to *agape*.

Christian love *(agape)* is the antithesis of worldly hate, but it is much more; it is the antithesis also of worldly love *(eros)* in all its forms. The gods of our time are but brittle images of *eros*-love. Unregenerate man fashions and worships these because they gratify subjective ambitions, and reflect therefore man's desire to control or to manipulate the universe for selfish ends. The fact that God is love (I John 4:16), that the Creator is *agape*, means that human nature originally and essentially should be understood and judged from the standpoint not of *eros* but of *agape*. Barth rightly emphasizes that *agape* "has its basis in the good being and action of God," and *eros* "in the corruption of man" (*Church Dogmatics*, Edinburgh, T. & T. Clark, 1958, IV/2, p. 747). The theories of Machiavelli, Hobbes, Darwin, and Dewey, who begin with the beast-nature of man and try to superimpose on this a devout-nature, are thoroughly false. The prospect of abiding social order cannot be predicated upon fallen *eros*-love, but comes only through man's regeneration by and to *agape*-love.

Since the coming of Jesus Christ into this world, God's standard of neighbor love is clear and unmistakable, for He is the incarnation of untarnished *agape*-love. Jesus Christ is the one loved of God, the one who perfectly loves the Father, and who identified Himself with human nature to give Himself completely and selflessly for His fellowman. Again and again the epistles exhort us to a ministry "even as Christ . . ." whose great example crowds the Gospels.

Jesus Christ is the original personification of all Christian action. In Him we see the new and true man, the completely sanctified man who lives by and in the Spirit. Only such life in the Spirit can yield and explain Christian love.

It is Jesus Christ's incomparable love and the astounding love of the early Christians that enticed civilized peoples in their humanitarian attempts to transform *eros* into *agape*. Despite its modern secular perspective, the Western world still bears in its history innumerable and ineradicable traces of the Biblical virtues and their condemning force. It is quite understandable that unregenerate man, stranger though he is to *agape,* should aspire to cultivate some of *agape*'s fruits from *eros*. Consequently we see the remarkable phenomenon of a secular society trying to harvest hope, peace, and love (as more-than-*eros*) from unregenerate human nature. Although temporarily inspired and influenced by broken fragments of Christian virtue, such secular efforts must necessarily lapse again into *eros,* because men in bondage to sin have not been truly liberated and livened to love.

The present theological and spiritual delinquency of secular society has similarly invaded today's Christian community and compromised the role of *agape* in the professing Church. Even when a formally proper view of the love of God is preserved—God's for man and man's for God—the social application of *agape* is often distorted into something *erotico*-humanistic. Such futile attempts to superimpose Christian virtue upon unregenerate human nature then come to characterize even the Church, as in recent Western Protestantism. Influenced by Kant and Ritschl, the Church tried to identify rationalistic moralism or humanitarian love for others with love to God. Some American Protestant enthusiasts for social action still tend to err in this direction; whatever doctrine of God they may uphold on the horizon of this humanitarian concern serves to reinforce rather than motivate the content of social activism. Viewed apart from love for God or as the sole and exhaustive expression of love for God, such social activity has no standing as Christian obedience. Detached from the history of salvation it may even be comprehended as an expression of self-love and a form of spiritual disobedience. The Church, unfortunately, often adopts *eros*-sponsored objectives and acts on *eros* rather than *agape* motivations. Even where it avoids these errors and retains an awareness of the uniqueness of *agape,* the Church may honor *agape* more in pious tribute and emotional attachment than in practical expression.

Insofar as the professing Church is unregenerate and hence a stranger to the power of true love, it should surprise no one that it conceives its mission to be the Christianizing of the world rather than the evangelizing of mankind, and that it relies on other than supernatural dynamic for its mission in the world. Even ecclesiastical leaders cannot rely on a power they have never experienced. What is surprising, however, is the extent to which evangelical Christians are deployed into assisting social programs which are poorly defined and motivated from the Biblical perspective.

It is true, of course, that even the devout individual believer is tempted always to lapse into *eros*-love and must daily rely on the Spirit to fire and maintain *agape*-love. Even so, it is possible for the believer while he offers and gives his means to withold himself from God and his fellow-men. In *agape*-love is he not to emulate God's love as displayed in the crucifixion? While the believer is no deity and therefore cannot embody *agape* in its fullness and perfection, neverthless he is able to manifest the *agape* of the new creature in Christ the incarnate *agape*. Thereby

God's nature and action as the living fount of love will bear decisively on all areas of social tension in our times. It is this illuminating dynamic which empowers the regenerate body of Christ with fresh vigor in the sin-darkened world.

Is not love meaningless if its true center is theoretically known and preserved but never radiates outward to enfold its needy object? Dare we criticize those who respond to areas of need in the spirit of *eros*, if we never bring to these same areas the *agape* we know and herald? Is *agape* any longer really *agape* if it is intention only, and not also action? Is God's Lamb a lamb slain only in eternity? Is not Christ's death on the Cross the supreme proof of God's love? The conjoining of "God and neighbor" in the Christian's love-imperative assures us that *agape* is to be applied in the world even as Jesus entered the stream of history and ministered. If the Christian does not demonstrate the transforming power of *agape* in the world, if his life falsifies and betrays the very spiritual realities he affirms by merely duplicating what is elsewhere attained and visible, will not the world quite understandably ignore the claims made for *agape*-love?

The Christian's obligation to *neighbor*-love and Christ's commission to *make* disciples define social concern in terms of personal responsibility. This Biblical exposition of social concern in the context of believer to neighbor is neither accidental nor incidental but essential. It prevents his hallowing merely general or impersonal causes and correlates his devotion to principles with a devotion to persons, first of all to the Godhead and then to the individuals around him. This Biblical emphasis on neighbor is especially important in an age when social reformers often seek the welfare of humanity in general but neglect specific neighbor-relations.

Any program of social ethics is suspect, therefore, if it dulls the Christian passion to evangelize the lost, or attaches the Christian's hope for transforming society to any other dynamic than that of spiritual regeneration. Christian social action, accordingly, is no mere program of propaganda, resolution, or legislation which imposes scriptural ideals upon the confused world of unregenerate men. The Christian is obligated, of course, to protest injustice, protect human rights before the law, and promote justice. He has no mandate to legislate "Christian love" upon unregenerate society, however, for such love is a gift that must be voluntarily accepted. Only the Christian who has experienced God's redemptive love knows the secret of displaying true neighbor-love. To think that enlistment and dedication of the unregenerate to "universal 'love' for mankind" is a special victory for the Christian Church is indeed to be deceived. Such error merely weakens the true import of *agape* and levies excessive and impossible expectations upon *eros*. The Christian mission to society must both proclaim Jesus Christ as Saviour and Lord and distinguish between *agape* and *eros*.

In the tussle of modern society, science is probing the stellar world with doomsday weapons; political tyranny already controls the destinies of eight million persons; current literary and propaganda techniques portray merely limpid man-made gods. Only the God who shows Himself remains the abiding victor over the struggles of time and space. He alone is the competent Wayshower in a world blinded by irrationalism, sullied by sin, perverted by power, and overgrown with hate. Christ the manifested Wisdom of God puts our puny rationalizations to rout. Christ the Word become flesh shuts us up either to repentance or to doom. Christ the Holy Lord marks the Kingdoms of this world for His judgment and disposition. Yet Christ, the crucified

but everliving, incomparable Lover, is able to banish the
seething hatred of our present spiteful age, and must indeed
banish it in the age to come.

Chapter II

THE GOSPEL AND THE GRAPEVINE

In the tense days of the Civil War, rumors about military strategy and troop movements flashed like lightning between the opposing forces. Since these reports often were sensational fabrications, a special term was coined to describe them. They came, it was said, by "grapevine telegraph."

For better or worse the grapevine—or the world of rumor —still exercises an immense influence on people's lives. Propagandists exploit the mass media and the market place for special purposes. Yet the "grapevine telegraph" can carry good news as well as false hopes, and we cannot afford to overlook its importance.

In Washington, D.C., an employee of the U.S. State Department was reminiscing one day about his special assignment after World War II. Together with associates he was sent to troublespots around the world to analyze the main discontents of the people. His own particular task was among the Indians of the Andes mountains, an area of considerable ferment. It was there this government worker made an unexpected discovery, one that left an indelible impression upon him. In a surprising number of those distant and primitive Indian homes, he found two pictures on the walls. One, and this was not surprising, was a halo-encircled image of Jesus of Nazareth in the Roman Catholic tradition. The other—and this was the shocker—was a picture of Franklin Delano Roosevelt.

The remarkable thing—and it was remarkable—was that the grapevine had penetrated even to these remote Indians with the message that President Roosevelt was somehow identified with their personal discontents. The picture of Roosevelt was displayed not simply because of shrewd political propaganda. Rather, to these dissatisfied, miserable Indians it spoke of a man who somehow cared about their problems.

As I listened to this report, I couldn't help wondering whose picture animates those Indian homes today. That of Karl Marx, perchance? I forewent that question because another implication of my friend's discovery troubled me more. Why, in our day, doesn't the grapevine carry to the masses—as it did in the first century—the good news of man's deliverance by Jesus Christ alone? Why, in addition to the surviving awareness of Jesus, do so many people need a second picture? Why is it that where the recognition of Jesus survives He is so widely regarded in the category of a religious lightning rod or good luck charm? Why does the grapevine today commit modern man in his basic needs and discontents to deliverers other than the Holy One of Nazareth?

First century Palestine, occupied by the Romans, and seething from time to time with the spirit of revolt, must have echoed with many soaring reports. Yet among those flashes of news none was more spectacular and sensational than word about one Jesus of Nazareth. "This rumor of him," writes Luke (referring to the report that "a great prophet is risen up among us" and that "God hath visited his people")—this rumor "went forth throughout all the region round about" (Luke 7:16-17). And Mark, com-

menting on the very beginning of Jesus' ministry, notes
that "at once his fame spread everywhere throughout all
the surrounding region of Galilee" (Mark 1:28). In that
generation when Jesus Christ appeared among men incarnate, crucified and risen, the grapevine telegraph flashed
new hope to countless multitudes; to those whose daily
existence languished in the dust of death, it offered the
high promise of new life.

In our own century the underground seldom pulses
with this good news of redemption in Christ Jesus. Why?
Why does a Hitler or a Khrushchev or a Mao Tse-tung
spark illusory hopes of a new and better day in the hearts
of millions, while our own lives as a commentary on the
deeds and words of Jesus inspire so little and so few? How
ought the Christian task force—you and I included—to
identify with modern men in their discontents so that
people will be encouraged once again to seek Christian
solutions? How ought we Christians to relate ourselves to
the dissatisfied throngs so they will probe the Christian
answer?

A hundred times in past months I have put this question
to myself, and to missionaries and teachers on foreign fields
—in Africa, in Europe, and in the Middle East. Hoping to
sharpen the cutting edge of Christian witness in these dis-
traught times, I have asked it over and over, sometimes of a
lonely worker at some distant outpost, sometimes in large
group conversations in a foreign city.

I. Our Identification With Christ Must Be Clear

In modern times Christianity has come to mean a great
many things. Christendom is no longer marked by an
apostolic unity of faith and doctrine. In almost every city
in the modern world one prominent spokesman's version
of the Christian faith is contradicted by another's. Chris-

tianity is offered to the world as the one true religion, yet
those who claim to be Christians seem to cancel out each
other's views of the essential content of revealed religion.

Happily, more and more pulpits and religious publications
address this problem of the Church's identification with
Christ, and it needs to be faced even more earnestly. We
can hardly expect the world to comprehend what identification with Christ means while those who call themselves
Christians remain conspicuously divided over its nature.

It is great gain that most religious bodies are now speaking to each other instead of persecuting or slandering each
other. But the ecumenical movement has not dispelled widespread uncertainty over the essence of Christian religion.
The merging of churches does not settle the question of
what is intellectually tolerable or intolerable as a statement
of historic Christianity. In facing the modern world the
prime problem of contemporary Christianity is not the
unfortunate proliferation of denominations but the unbear-
able divergence over the truth of revelation perpetuated by
the hydra-headed ecumenical colossus. No verbal glorifying
of the "coming world church" can skim the theological
differences not only between Protestanism and Eastern
Orthodoxy and Roman Catholicism, but within the denominations themselves. Is it really a secondary concern of
identification with Christ and of Christian unity whether
the Pope is Christ's authorized viceregent on earth or simply
the most presumptive of ecclesiastics? In Europe Rudolf
Bultmann's existentialism has demeaned the New Testament miracles into myths and attempted to destroy any
historical ground of Christian faith. Is it really a matter
of indifference to Christian unity and to identification with
Christ whether seminarians are schooled in speculation and
whether pulpits are haunted by heresy?

Evangelicals have always concentrated attention on the

meaning of identification with Christ, as well as with His body the Church, because multitudes hold deformed views of the Saviour and of the Christian faith. Moreover, in Israel, and Egypt, and Russia, and Congo, and South Africa, and Spain the problem of identification with Christ and His body takes a special direction and calls for special study.

II. Our Identification With People Must Be Clear

No less urgent, however, is the parallel problem of our Christian identification with the people. Alongside our vertical relationship to Christ, what of our horizontal relationship to mankind? Human ambitions are cresting, human longings are exploding, and multitudes everywhere grasp every fleeting propaganda promise of utopia on earth. How shall we Christian believers identify ourselves with the discontented multitudes so they do not ignore Christian answers? How relate ourselves to the restless masses to encourage a pursuit of Christian solutions?

1. Some frontier missionaries insist that effective identification with non-Christians requires "going native"—that is, adopting the *social customs* of those we aim to win. Speak the native language, eat native chop, wear native clothes, and live as the natives do, these Christian workers contend, and barriers to communication fall away. A generation after my father-in-law's death in the Africa Cameroun, Bakweri natives gratefully served us peanut soup and palm chop such as he enjoyed in their homes while he witnessed of the Saviour. But to gain the confidence of nationals in our day missionaries seldom need to divorce themselves from Western customs except where Communist propagandists besmirch them as agents of "the imperial West." Most nationals are more interested in Western science and industry than in the Gospel. Nobody can, or wants to, turn back

the clock on the industrial revolution or the explosion of scientific learning.

Yet the retention of Western ways seems to summon nationals to a new culture as well as to a new religion, thus interposing an unnecessary obstacle to faith. Christianity does not call men first to decision for Western culture and then to decision for Christ. There is live danger of transplanting Western materialistic discontents and, in the name of evangelism, superimposing them on others. Missionaries should consider carefully the discontents they create in the lives of those to whom they minister. Does their Christian witness unwittingly shape material idols and encourage interest in "the good life" which has more in common with a secular doctrine of comfort than with the spiritual ministry of the Comforter? In Southern Rhodesia some missionaries housed an "indigenous church" of African believers in an attractive new building. When gifts to the building fund lagged, missionaries exerted pressures for funds. The nationals protested that they would rather worship God outdoors under the trees as was their custom. Was it Biblical principle or Western tradition, we might ask, that moved their worship inside an attractive building whose cost they could not carry?

We Americans readily materialize the Biblical "God of all comfort" into a reflex of our gadget-culture. In my college days a campus coed told her classmates that she would be willing to go to Africa as a missionary only if she could take along a refrigerator. In some locations it would take a remarkably long electric cord to keep it running. As far as I know, she ended up not on a mission field, but with a refrigerator. Some years ago I met a seminary graduate who had lapsed from his call to the ministry and had become an appliance salesman. He informed me that he was now "preaching the gospel of refrigerators."

Do we infect others with our Western preoccupation with creature comforts? I vividly recall an experience in the Philippine Islands after a turbulent flight from Baguio with a World Vision pastors' conference team. In Iloilo we found bleak hotel accommodations. A tiny room and toilet-shower cubicle became the "home for a week" that saintly Pastor Kyung Chik Han of Seoul and I were to share. That gallant minister had led a small army of anxious believers out of North Korea ahead of the advancing Communists. Along the way they buried the aged and the infants who could not endure the hardships of the escape route. Upon reaching Seoul in South Korea the survivors built new homes and a new place of worship, where today Pastor Han numbers his Sunday churchgoers in the thousands.

A swift glance at our meager Iloilo lodgings told me more than I wanted to know: two small bed cots, a tiny wooden chair built for a diminutive Filipino (not for an overstuffed American), and a rickety table (without a lamp) too small to support even a trim piece of luggage. When Pastor Han spoke up just as I was preparing to do so, I realized that he too had appraised the situation but, as it developed, had reached a verdict very different from my own. "You take the chair and the table, Brother Henry," he said softly; "I'm used to the very simple things of life."

In those few words I sensed that he and I were living in two very different worlds. Three times Han had lost everything he owned to the Communists; in his eyes this despised chair and shaky table seemed to be luxuries. So the emphasis on "going native" is a wholesome protest against carrying too much bag and baggage with the Gospel, and thereby confusing people about its essence. But we are not always called to identify ourselves with all social customs of others in order to reach them with the Gospel.

2. Sometimes the plea for "cultural identification" with others takes another turn, and urges our uncritical adoption also of the reigning *social vices,* lest we interpose parochial negations as a secondary barrier to faith. It is highly regrettable indeed, that Christianity is sometimes misunderstood as mere abstinence from drinking and smoking and dancing, and not as God's free offer of salvation. Those who indulge are then disposed to face the question of decision for or against Christ on the wrong level.

A leading Latin American missionary once told me of his utter frustration because, when he identified himself as evangelical, three times out of five the response was, "Oh, you are one of those folks that don't drink or smoke." Now in our society alcoholism is undeniably a pernicious cultural vice, and medical science attests the incompatibility of cigarette-addiction with a Christian regard for the dignity of the human body; avoidance of these habits therefore has sound supportive principles.

But when the public narrowly misunderstands Christianity in terms of cultural negation, rather than in terms of the evangelical Gospel, the effective presentation of Christ is hindered, and we encourage a rejection of Christ through this misunderstanding. Yet this situation is ideally corrected not by locating Christianity on the side of dubious personal vices, but by keeping the nature of the Gospel in clear view. Neither our connection with social custom nor our disconnection with social vice is to constitute an obstacle to the Gospel.

3. How then ought we to be identified with men and women of the world so they will seek Christian solutions? Surely it would be a grave mistake to seek to win men and women to Christ by identifying ourselves uncritically with their *social discontents.* However attractive that option has become in the twentieth century, the grave error of the

modernist "social gospel" lay precisely in its deployment of Biblical social concern into the service of merely secular aspirations. Jesus rebuked the preoccupation of the multitudes with perishable bread, and had to warn even His own disciples against this temptation.

The dissatisfactions of unregenerate man lack a spiritual quality, as do his satisfactions. Complaints against the emptiness of life are often obscure, and easily given false labels. The African protesting the "white man's domination" may really want material betterment however he gets it. The wealthy African is not beyond exploiting the poor African, and greater differences actually exist within the races than between the races. The Gospel must not be tapered to unspiritual aspirations whereby religion is made a mere instrument of personal or social gratification.

One can anticipate the rejoinder of liberal-minded churchmen. Refuse to identify yourself with the social discontents of the masses, they say, and you only "talk past" them, not "to" them. So Christianity forfeits its relevance in the social arena, it is argued, and allows Marxism or some other *ism* exclusive rights to address political and economic discontents.

On first hearing, this may sound credible. But it does not stand the test of Biblical theology and ethics. For this "social gospel" obscures the fact of personal sin and guilt, and the need of personal redemption; it is unsure of the identity of the Lord of the Church, of Biblical dynamisms, and of authentic Christian solutions. All the modern isms *exploit* the vacuums in human life in the interest of their alien ideologies; they do not really address men realistically and relevantly, but in fact "talk past" them as persons. They are interested in changing man's environment, but not in transforming men.

Portugal is a land of growing economic discontent because of its pronounced disparity between the few families of vast wealth and multitudes with little of this world's goods. To Protestant workers in Lisbon, I put my persistent question in the most provocative way: "How ought the Christian task force to identify itself with the discontents of the Portuguese people so they will seek Christian solutions?" A veteran evangelical leader met the question head-on: "That way of putting it has revolutionary implications. We are not called upon to identify ourselves with the discontents of the people, but with their needs." His discerning comment stressed a distinction of basic importance. The next night in Portugal's second city, Porto, I addressed the same question to the evangelical task force there. An evangelist promptly asked the pastors and workers to sing their widely-used evangelistic "theme song": "More Than a Millionaire." While speaking of God's care for man's legitimate needs, it warned also against the inadequacy of the material; whoever finds Christ discovers that treasure without which even millionaires remain paupers. As one recent convert put it, "the 'have nots' sometimes have more than the 'haves'!"

4. To the *needs* of people, then, in distinction from their wants, Christians are divinely obliged to relate themselves. We must relate ourselves to needs of neighbors, those "at our side," as an immediate responsibility. This is the essence of the Good Samaritan: he responds to the needs of his neighbor, and his neighbor is whoever crosses his path.

We cannot, of course, relate ourselves to all needs of all people; we cannot cope even with all needs of all neighbors. But our inescapable obligation is to minister to *survival needs* at very least—drink for the the thirsty; food for the hungry; raiment for the destitute; special care for the orphans, the afflicted, and the widows in need; and concern for those in prison.

5. Not even with men's needs as such are we required to identify ourselves, as much as with *persons* besieged by needs and discontents.

To identify oneself with persons while withholding himself from those many causes and programs which today are venerated as mechanical saviors and redeemers is not always easy, since the multitudes respond swiftly to sociopolitical programs that promise utopia. In many lands revolutionary subversive agitators have promoted widespread mistrust of the white man's faltering efforts at "identification." White missionaries may move from African hut to hut rubbing shoulders with nationals, eating their food, learning their language, entering into their trials, only to be followed by political radicals who viciously discredit these Christian workers as advocates of white domination and black suppression, and as champions of the *status quo*. But there are also sounder reasons for African doubts.

In Rhodesia even national Christians privately picture white missionaries as "native commissioners" (a term borrowed from colonial administration) because they meet them only at their desk, and view them as foreign representatives who manipulate the people as mere religious digits for organizational purposes. Nor is the ecumenical "organization man" the only transgressor in encouraging this feeling that Christians are not as much interested in persons as in statistics. In South Africa an American flies his missionary plane dropping Gospels of John over rural areas to scarcely visible people below. If these South Africans can read English, they have attended schools requiring Bible study, and such wholesale distribution is superfluous; if they cannot, the distribution is senseless. What becomes of personal identification in such activity?

"For forty years," said a missionary in Liberia, "this has

been my missionary rule: If an African comes, always turn aside and listen. You can't help people while you stand on a stepladder and they must gaze up; you must come down. The African is a supersensitive somebody. He knows when you love him and when you don't." In Monrovia, a Christian worker and former high official in the Liberian Information Service, suggested a simple test: "Does the white man meet Africans only at the front door, or talk to them only on the rear piazza? Or are they sometimes invited inside to sit on the chairs?" She described a white missionary whose single act had permanently established her personal identification with all the Liberian believers. How so? At a child's funeral, the white missionary had stopped to kiss the mourning Negro mother, and inescapably identified herself in a common bond of humanity.

Along the west coast of Africa the "extended family system" prevails. When anybody finds a job, his unemployed relatives are all free to descend upon him for food and lodging—and they unhesitatingly do so. Some young Africans wonder therefore whether unemployment or employment is the greater blessing. Sometimes even Christian concern is put to an awkward test in the face of such expectations. Assigned to a United Nations project a Nigerian worker arrived in Lagos (where hotel rates are exorbitant) a full day ahead of his assignment. He presented himself to the project director, a Methodist layman, with a plea for lodging. When the director pointed out that the worker had arrived early, the African replied, "Then you don't care whether I have a place to sleep or not." The director inquired, "Will any of your relatives or friends provide lodging overnight?" When the worker said he was unsure, the director decided to promote initiative and self-reliance, while preserving his sensitivity to human need. "If no friend in Lagos will give you lodging," he said, "come back and

I will take you in this evening." The worker found lodging, but the incident had its aftermath a week later, when this African worker publicly sang the praises of the U.N. project director who had invited him home for the night if none of his friends would meet his need. Here was person-to-person identification free of shallow sentiment.

The legitimate needs of persons are twofold: *social justice* and *redemptive love*.

These are also man's "survival needs." The Church is learning the hard way that it must not be indifferent to any denial of equal treatment to persons before the law. Above all, Christians claim, the Gospel preserves the high dignity of human existence. But what of the churchgoer who engages in "Jewish evangelism week" to bring into church membership Hebrews whom he has under no circumstances wanted to have as neighbors? Or of the churchgoer who lacks indignation over racial discrimination at home, while he enthusiastically promotes missions in Africa? Are not men and women thereby encouraged to misunderstand Christianity as a religion indifferent to the cleft in the body of mankind, and therefore as lacking in sensitivity over the dignity and rights of human beings?

Social justice is due, of course, not from Christians only, but from every man. And by no means have Christians generally been indifferent to social justice; indeed, the history of religion confirms the judgment that revealed religion (the ethical monotheism of the Bible) has yielded the profoundest insights into the nature and need of social justice as well as into the nature and need of personal redemption.

All civil government carries the obligation to preserve human equality before the law. Social justice can be sustained only through just government. Because the early Christians lived in a context of Roman jurisprudence, the Apostle Paul by appealing to his Roman citizenship and

the rights it implied before the law could protect himself
from Jewish religious intolerence and hatred. But no full
manifestation of social justice will emerge on earth until
Jesus Christ returns. If men were to wait for complete social
justice before they give the Gospel a hearing, they would
find themselves consigned to hell by their own injustices and
neglect of the Gospel. The millennium is future, but the day
of salvation is *now*—and no man dare ignore its offer of
personal redemption and spiritual renewal. Yet Christians
dare not cut men off from the body of humanity while they
seek to include them in the body of Christ. While social
justice is a legitimate need, the man of the world—whether
Jew or Gentile, black or white or yellow—needs also to be
reminded that redemptive love is an indispensable need,
and nothing excuses his failure to seek God's forgiving
grace.

If the sensitive social issues are often only skin-deep, the
problems of the whole man reach to the heart. That fact
drives missionaries on and on around the globe. In Central
Africa, Rhodesian missionaries were about to pay one of
their frequent calls on rural natives in a center of political
agitation, despite efforts by radicals to impugn their motives.
At the entrance to a hut a child's announcement voiced the
glad welcome of the parents inside: "Our white people
have come!" That interracial welcome is the hopeful antithesis to the revolutionary's provocation of interracial tension. The good news of the Gospel becomes the answer to
ugly political propaganda, and personal evangelism is vindi-
cated over against personal exploitation.

With the need of the whole person, not merely with
fragmentary aspects of the whole, we are to identify ourselves. Even a ministry predicated simply on "survival" needs
must reach beyond the material. Man is more than animal.
Not even repeated doses of aspirin, tranquilizers and bar-

biturates quell his spiritual hungers. His deepest needs stem from separation from God. He stands guilty before the Ten Commandments, and the Sermon on the Mount unmasks him as a miserable sinner. His own conscience approves Paul's indictment: "We all come short of the glory of God."

6. The Gospel of Christ speaks to the whole panorama of human requirements. Jesus began his public ministry with the majestic declaration: "The Spirit of the Lord is upon me, because he hath anointed me to preach the gospel to the poor; he hath sent me to heal the broken hearted, to preach deliverance to the captives, and recovering of sight to the blind, to set at liberty them that are bruised, to preach the acceptable year of the Lord" (Luke 4:18-19).

As His followers we too are to identify ourselves *with God's discontents with humanity and with God's desires for humanity.* To the Congo, missionaries came preaching, teaching, and healing—as did the early disciples—and as they penetrated the African bush they built churches, schools, and hospitals seeking the redemption of the whole man. In those jungles dark with fear, treachery, and witchcraft, they summoned their new neighbors in need to the high prospect of a redeemed soul, informed mind, and consecrated body—in short, to renewal in the image of God.

"Thou art Simon; thou shalt be called Cephas"—so Jesus' promise echoes still to man in his discontents and needs (John 1:42). "Except a man be born again, he cannot see the kingdom of God" (John 3:3). "Seek ye first the kingdom of heaven and all these things will be added unto you" (Matthew 6:33). The God of creation and judgment, of grace and glory, sifted man's legitimate needs from illegitimate desires; divine regeneration honed the sense of sin and the sense of righteousness to new sharpness. Those who knew the Lord of glory now set their affections "on things above" (Colossians 3:2), and the new life they found in Christ Jesus was so exceedingly rewarding that their former existence seemed but a living death.

The nature of true hope was now clear: only the resurrection of Christ carried hope for a doomed and dying race. "If Christ be not risen. . . . faith is vain" wrote Paul (I Corinthians 15:14). Peter wrote of men "begotten again unto a living hope" (I Peter 1:3), and the author of Hebrews mirrored "the bringing in of a better hope" (Hebrews 7:19). Men were no longer like warriors fighting without a helmet; "for an helmet" they now had "the hope of salvation" (I Thessalonians 5:8). They had become "prisoners of hope" so that even in their grief they no longer sorrowed "as those who have no hope" (I Thessalonians 4:13). They were a race apart, a new race of men. Once they lacked hope and were without God in the world (Ephesians 2:2), but now they were to "be ready to give to every man a reason of the hope" that was in them (I Peter 3:15), Christ had risen, and therefore hope had risen once again in the hearts of men.

How can we today provoke our own generation to grasp the unsuspected meaning of these truths and to appropriate the great power of these realities? Its baseless hopes and empty faiths swiftly fade away. Why then do not the men of our time hear our shout of joy, from hearts that once shared their false delusions? How can the Christian community recover that apostolic spontaneity that staggered the pagan world by its sheer power and purity? Those early Christians were poised for martyrdom rather than to silence the proclamation of the Word—are we? They stood ready to disobey tyrants to preach a Gospel without which men are lost forever—do we? They so lived in the holy presence of God that their daily deeds and words were an undeniable apologetic for the supernatural world—do we?

Today the grapevine stirs with excitement. It bristles with news of photographs of the moon and projected landings there, of new intercontinental missiles, of men walking in space, of science standing on the bridge between the non-living and the living, of the atomic era moving us into a new dimension of civilization, and so on. Why does the grapevine buzz with the news of other rescuers, and so seldom mention Him whose messengers we are?

On our train traveling from the East German border to Nürnberg we conversed with the elderly couple in our compartment, refugees from Sudetenland which the Russians had occupied. In the difficult days of suffering under Russian occupation their dwindling hope was kept alive by reports that if only they could make it to the Bavarian frontier, the American military would help them. They recalled how, when they could scarcely take the last steps, the American soldiers met them. Nor would they forget the first Care package—after all these years they could still taste the portions of turkey it offered. The fact that Americans cared had nourished their fading hope that life might again seem worthwhile.

The assassination of President Kennedy occurred while we were half a world away. The evening after that dread event we were stopped in South Africa on the streets of Johannesburg—one of the world's most segregated cities— by a Negro in his middle twenties. "You are Americans?" he asked cautiously. My wife and I proudly owned his identification. "Well," he continued insistently, "what hope remains for us, if *that* can happen in your country?" Misled by some of the early radio reports, this young Bantu linked Mr. Kennedy's assassination to his strong stand on civil rights. Yet one remarkable fact could not be gainsaid. Thousands of miles from American shores, a spokesman for the younger generation of Negroes in South Africa had

clearly pinned his hopes for a new day of racial dignity to
Mr. Kennedy's star. Half way around the world the grapevine was stirring.

Do you think the grapevine can any more pulsate with
news that "the people that walked in darkness have seen
a great light"; that the Prince of Peace is come and offers
reconciliation to a race in ruin; that the risen Christ grants
forgiveness of sins and life fit for eternity to all who own
Him as Saviour and Lord; that He will come again to rule
in righteousness over the nations; that He is—as another has
expressed it well—"this world's last, best, and only hope"?
I ask you: can the Church of Jesus Christ once again set
the hearts of men singing with the prospect of this new
and living hope? Has the Gospel lost its power to inspire
man's longing for abundant life? Can the joys of Christian
experience still provoke the lost to covet life's best gifts?

Are we to abandon our contemporaries through defeatism
and despair, on the ground that our post-Christian century
has turned its back finally and irrevocably upon the cross?
Or that the modern world of mass communication and
propaganda is the special province of Antichrist? Do we
yield only to earlier generations the vision that inspired
songs of faith like "From Greenland's icy mountains to
India's coral strands. . . ."?

Would throngs ever have started to move toward the
great evangelistic crusades in our generation had Billy
Graham reconciled himself to one such spiritual retreat
after another? Would evangelical forces have had a rally-
ing medium like *Christianity Today* if devout laymen had
decided that human history had now bypassed all possibility
of effective spiritual decision? The grapevine telegraph is
not closed down to Christians on any continent. What are
we doing to get it stirring with the fame and rumor of
Christ?

When believers in Guatemala organized regional prayer meetings for Evangelism in Depth, news of their spiritual concern to win neighbors for Christ spread so contagiously that hundreds were saved before any crusade got underway. The grapevine telegraph was carrying the "good news" in Latin America.

In Greece, where one is virtually born Greek Orthodox, the grapevine has been stirring also. The Free Evangelical Church has sprung into being with thousands of members. I asked a leading layman high in Greek government councils what strategy accounted for its phenomenal growth into thirty-nine churches. "Strategy?" he repeated, with an air of surprise. "We had a real experience in the results of prayer. God so blessed us that others dared not disbelieve in the miracles of God. We became a menace to those who did not believe, and who held themselves aloof from these blessings." That is the New Testament way to set the grapevine stirring again in our own day and age.

Chapter III

INVOLVEMENT ON CONTEMPORARY FRONTIERS

If Christian involvement in the world is truly an evangelical imperative—and, properly understood, I believe it is —then it must be comprehended within our Lord's commission, "As the Father hath sent me, so send I you." Jesus was the only Redeemer sent into the world for the salvation of sinners; He was the first Evangelist compassionately proclaiming an already accomplished atonement; He was the foremost Exemplar mixing with men and recalling humanity to a high and holy destiny. Our staggering task as Christian believers is to evangelize this world and to teach men all that Jesus has commanded. Since the Gospel challenges modern man in the totality of his existence, this commission we can hardly fulfill comprehensively unless we relate the Gospel to modern thought and to modern life, hence to contemporary philosophy, society and culture.

Two theological dangers overarch the evangelical effort to carry out this task.

One would relate Christianity primarily to social structures, and strip the Gospel of its imperative call to personal redemption by Jesus Christ who forgives sinners one by one and allots them individually a place in His kingdom. This interest simply in Christian culture or Christian civilization has plagued Western Christianity in modern as well as medieval times. In effect, it reduces the Gospel to a social philosophy and turns the Bible into an ideology, prizing them simply as instruments of social renovation. In my *Aspects of Christian Social Ethics* I urged that the Christian message to the world be subsumed in its entirety under the proclamation of Jesus Christ as Saviour and Lord, and that the Christian message to the social order remain firmly attached to that proclamation. It is quite proper and necessary to see Jesus as the Divine Evangelist, as the Divine Redeemer, as the Divine Lord, but it is something else again to see Him simply as a Divine Sociologist—as an architect of social justice and world order whose message and mission of personal redemption are secondary and dispensable.

The other temptation is to taper our proclamation of Jesus Christ solely to the message of individual redemption, to the forgiveness of sins, and to conceal the fact that He is the King of truth and the Lord of life. If it is objectionable to reduce the Gospel to a social ideology, it is no less objectionable to neglect and narrow the whole counsel of God by not affirming the lordship of Christ over the larger world of human learning and culture. The Christian community is divinely obliged to press a divine claim upon the nations of the earth and upon society, including all the power structures through whose techniques of constraint and compulsion the world seeks peace and order and justice.

The terrible cost of theological suppression or neglect of either aspect of this spiritual claim upon every arena of human decision is far greater than its truant arbiters realize. To withhold the Gospel from any person is to expose him to the perils of a Christless eternity and to rob him of the possibility of his recovery of the lost meaning and worth of personal existence. To withhold God's declarations in respect to man's social existence—the divine basis of justice, the divine sanction of human rights, the divine stipulation of human duties, the divine purpose for the state, the divine responsibility of human life and learning—is to withhold from the world a lively sense of that absolute standard by which men and nations will finally be judged, and by which they ought even now to be judging themselves.

It is to its credit that evangelical Christianity in America has kept alive a burden of evangelism and missions that has won the high esteem of Protestant Christianity around the world. In contrast to non-Protestant traditions and even to some segments of Protestantism, an evangelistic and missionary sensitivity distinguishes conservative Protestantism in America. Some of us share the credit quite unworthily, for even in our conservative churches only a minority truly carries the effective financial and prayer support of the evangelistic and missionary task. I cannot forget an experience in Colombia, Latin America, when traveling a few years ago on a World Vision team. A lad in his early twenties—whose persecuted family had lost their lives for the Gospel's sake at the hands of bigoted religious fanatics—one day approached me with a message for American Christians. "Thank them for me," he said, brokenly, "for sending missionaries so I could hear the Gospel and come to know Jesus Christ as my own Saviour." Would you not be embarrassed if I were to relay his gratitude to you personally? I concealed my own embarrassment, for I could recall no effort on my part that would have brought the good tidings within his reach. If we acknowledge that American Christianity has a noteworthy evangelistic vitality, which of us has reason to glory who almost daily is guilty of the sin of silence about the substitutionary death of Christ for sinners—whether in respect to downstreet neighbors or distant nationals? Not for nothing has *Christianity Today* sponsored a World Congress on Evangelism to sound the call "on with the task!"

On the other score—the relevant application of God's revelation to all the realms of human existence and energy—we have failed more conspicuously and even quite miserably. And this failure has had a repressive and retarding effect also upon our evangelistic message and activity, because through it the evangelical community tends to become isolated and ingrown in its associations, in its witness, and in its institutions.

Ingrown in its associations—until it feels that it is wicked simply to associate with the world, and in fact becomes pharisaical when it thinks itself pious. Ingrown in its associations—so that it no longer remembers or discovers what events and emotions stir and challenge the teeming multitudes, what grips their lives in the literature and music of the times, what characterizes the modern mind, or what defines the essence of existence for the very neighbors on our streets. Ingrown in its associations—so that it senses no challenge to formulate the Christian claim in terms that reflect its inescapable relevance to the contemporary man and to the problems of contemporary society.

Who is obligated more than the Christian intellectual to articulate Christ's claim for non-Christian intellectuals, professors for professors, pastors for rabbis, students for students —to reach across lines to "the outsider"? I do too little of it, and am embarrassed as I speak of it. Never do I fully rise above a sense of guilt about the unreached people around me. But of one thing I am wholly sure—for the man of learning as well as the man of action no message is more needed than the message of Jesus Christ. If you think the Gospel is only for the plebeian and not for the professional man, or only for the middle class suburbanite, and not for the laborer, nor for the politician, nor for the philosopher, nor for the man of the arts, you know only in a broken way what it is to be *sent* as Christ was sent. I would wither spiritually, I would think I were attending a funeral for my own spirit, could I not now and then at least press the claim of God upon the man who is consciously and deliberately identified with the modern mind.

I want you to know that I believe in the Apostles' Creed, and also the mandate to evangelize, and that despite my limited obedience and success in witnessing, I at least try. I believe in the necessary evangelization of the intellectual and professional class, and not only of the mission class and of the middle class. In our generation, too, Jesus Christ wants His Augustine and His Calvin—not simply brilliant students who know Augustine and Calvin inside out, but creative disciples who know the world outside and Christ inside and who can bring them together in an authentically Biblical, intellectually compelling, and spiritually powerful way.

Many of you fully agree, but you are somewhat disappointed over this concentration upon personal evangelism, and what may seem to condone a retreat from the larger social manifestation of Christianity and from the possibilities of Christian culture. Not at all. I have warned that ingrown association means an ingrown witness. And a subtle pharisaism soon "justifies" this lack of accessibility to the outsider, rationalizing it on grounds of the worldliness of the unbeliever and of the piety of the believer, when in fact that believer may now have manipulated and maneuvered himself outside the family of humanity because he can no longer courageously and winsomely contend with an alien mentality and with the spirit of his own age. Although the door remains open for broken spirits and anguished hearts to bring themselves under the preaching of the Gospel, the traffic between world and church then mainly moves one way insofar as it is spiritually venturesome: the church acts as if it has no longer been sent into the world, but wants the world to come insistently knocking at the door.

I do not, however, endorse the neo-orthodox notion that except for the church separate Christian organizations are manifestations of spiritual pride and that evangelical Christians ought never to promote separate movements such as Christian professional, business or labor associations, as if such organizations necessarily imply a shirking of evangelical responsibility in the world. Hence I disagree with the dogmatic disapproval of distinctively Christian movements voiced by Karl Barth (*Church Dogmatics* II/2, p. 721) and Emil Brunner (*The Divine Imperative,* pp. 432, 673). When Christians are such a small minority that their influence in secular circles is negligible, they can perhaps register that influence more effectively upon the world in a corporate way, particularly if they need opportunity to formulate their own perspectives on critical issues. This is one reason I continue to view the idea of a Christian university with favor, since it would train a dedicated task force of students to permeate the arena of secular education and to manifest the meaning of vocational Christian service.

Secular organizations, on the other hand, seldom require evangelicals to comply with Biblically prohibited positions. The complaint that secular agencies *per se* are based on anti-Christian principles, and inevitably commit their constituencies to practices irreconcilable with scriptural loyalties, or that because they officially ignore divine authority and exhibit neutrality toward Biblical emphases the believer is required in good conscience to shun them, rests upon a misunderstanding of the Christian's role in the world. The scriptural principle of separation does not require the establishment of "spiritual" versus "secular" organizations. There is no scriptural "social ethics" that demands separate socio-political organizations as ideal instruments of Christian strategy, and hence obliging believers to establish a completely "Christian" versus "non-Christian" front in the social realm, the economic realm, the political realm, and so on. The establishment of separate Christian movements is neither a matter of divine mandate nor divine prohibition but, as scholars like Herman Dooyeweerd and Henry Stob have had in recent years to remind their own Reformed constituencies, it is a question of responsible strategy, of prudence in view of contemporary circumstances.

In this case, then, we need to judge our already separately existing institutions by what their practical consequences are, not simply for the Church as such, but for the larger body of humanity. I have spoken at a Christian Business Men's Committee where the chairman told me that my appearance was the only time in twenty years that anybody had spoken on the Christian view of work. Today there is a world crisis in the realm of labor and economics—and we have a right to ask whether in our separate organizations Christian business men or laborers actually face these issues and authentically refract Christian perspectives into the social scene, or whether such concerns are wholly neglected for the otherwise quite legitimate and also indispensable task of personal evangelism.

One high price of evangelical isolation is that the high claim of God is insulated from the social structures of our day. No longer does the revelation of God challenge these social structures, and they do not dispute and contradict it, because they exist indifferently to it and can even ignore it. The result is alarming. Not only is the Gospel withheld from this larger world of culture and public life so that comparatively few leaders in strategic posts any longer know Christ, but worse yet, effective spiritual access to these formative minds is all but lost to the evangelical community. The general revelation of God that survives in sullied form in history and conscience is subordinated to the secular schemes on which world leaders rest the advancement of civilization and culture. Through its own virtual concealment of the powerful realities of revealed religion the Christian community meanwhile suppresses any reinforcement of divine truth and righteousness. The world outside of Christ is thus cut off from effective knowledge of that divine criterion which measures the worth of men and of nations. Yet the commandments of God not only constitute the standard by which mankind is to be judged at last, but they supply the only basis for a just and durable social order in our time and throughout history.

In our fulfillment of social responsibilities the New Testament does not require that we ask first whether men are Christians, and to be sure that they are, as the precondition of compassionate concern. Rather, the Bible affirms our human solidarity on the basis of man's creation and fall, as well as of man's prospect of redemption. The stimulated sense of the unity of the race, of universal neighborhood, of considerate concern for the whole of humanity, of the vision of social justice for all, belong to mature Christian manhood.

The eyes of the world were fixed on Britain by the death of Winston Churchill, eulogized as the greatest figure of the twentieth century. In those days of tribute in mourning, many devout believers whispered, "What loss that this man seemed to lack a personal faith in Christ; what tragedy that one who can lead a nation to victory in the supreme test of his generation should fail in the greatest of all tests. that of a confident destiny in eternity." But the question may equally well be turned the other way. For the greatness of Churchill lay in his identification with the people in their national needs. He won his way by making the cares of humanity critically and confidently his own. What loss that no sure Christian had compassion and courage and greatness to step into this vacuum; what tragedy that men who were ready to meet the supreme test of human destiny should leave their fellows so vulnerably exposed to the powers of antichrist in the lesser crises of human history.

Do not think that the penalties of this isolation are paid only by the world, and not at all by the evangelical community. When the Christian is sure only that Christ is the divine agent in the regeneration of believers—and the whole of Christian truth and life, and of God's relation to the universe and culture, reduces simply to "You ask me how I know he lives? He lives within my heart!"—the neglected areas of truth are soon inhabited by the secular spirits of our age, and these in turn rise to challenge the confidence of the Christian who erects his own spiritual experience on so narrow a strip of commitment. The evangelical who yields Genesis One and Three to evolutionary naturalism soon has trouble holding John One and Three for miraculous supernaturalism. A complete Biblical theology mirrors Jesus Christ as the divine agent in creation, in revelation, in redemption, in sanctification and in judgment, and it does not shrink from locating the foundations of morality in the will of God, nor from asserting the universal significance of revealed religion, nor from affirming the universality of Christ truth. The loss of these perspectives leads to cold and cruel negligence in the Christian's fulfillment of his larger responsibilities in the social order, and it rests on an abortive theology that nurtures a truncated religious experience replete with dichotomies, conflicts and repressions.

Here our Christian campuses bear great responsibility for helping to shape a spiritual maturity that reaches both to the changeless foundations of revealed religion and to the changing frontiers of a world in anguish. God desires from each of us an understanding of Him and of His purposes not as something merely inherited from a Christian home, not as something temporarily borrowed from the reserve reading shelves, but as a reality rooted in our own conviction and existence. A Christian home is a great asset, although some beneficiaries don't realize it until they are young marrieds; a reserve reading list is a great treasury, although some students don't realize it until they graduate, or until they don't. But a faith lacking in courage to face the world can thwart vital Christianity no less than does doctrinal delinquency.

To stand in one's own generation moved by a lively concern for the spiritual fate and eternal destiny of all men, to move among them with a sense of moral responsibility and mission, to engage in the common struggle for survival, to disclose the secret of life in one's own commitment, to mirror the content of justice, to demonstrate the lordship of Christ in worship and work and leisure, belong, as I see, it to the hard reality of being a Christian. The more richly a person lives in his generation, the less he will feel the *necessity* of isolating himself from his age, and the more comfortably he will be identified with people, however much he is distinguishable from them because he sees through their feelings and desires, and knows the fallacies of the modern mind, and confidently mirrors and reflects a sure solution to the fundamental problems of contemporary existence. For his every contact with the world is a freshly paved crossroads over which to carry a divine word and witness; and every intellectual sniper along the way becomes another prospect for a future audience on Mars Hill.

The very structures of social life, we have said, need to echo God's clarion call to responsible service. Among the social structures within which God created man is the order of labor and economics with its law of "work and eat."

Not only *that* man works but *what* he does and *when,* and *how* and *why* he does it, falls into the province of divine appointment and under divine scrutiny. If evangelical Christians have rightly avoided the wrong kinds of work, they have wrongly neglected many of the right vocations. Civilization and culture exist wholly as human possibilities. As spiritual manifestations of reason and volition and emotion, they either conform to the holy will of God or they become ambiguous instruments of the profane and demonic. So every talent becomes a call to the high service of God and man, a divine entrustment contributory to human welfare. And since God wills civil government for the preservation of justice, since He wills a just social and economic order in which human duties and human rights prevail, since in His providence He apportions diverse creative gifts to all men, each in his time and place is called to the fullest possible stewardship of abilities. The minister, the statesman, the physician, the teacher, the scientist, the lawyer, the banker, the artist—each and all are legitimate vocations that dare not be left to men for whom spiritual realities are optional or dispensable.

I shall not here repeat what already appears in other published writings that fully reflect my views. While I make no pretense of infallibility, one fact of which I am sure is that my dissatisfactions with our present stance in the world seek to advance a biblically-controlled view, not to displace it. When I wrote *The Uneasy Conscience of Modern Fundamentalism* almost twenty years ago, it was intended as a series of essays in a religious magazine. But the emphasis was thought to be so explosive that a publisher decided to get it into the hands of readers under a single cover, preferring one atomic detonation to a series of subnuclear blasts. *United Evangelical Action* responded gingerly; refusing to take sides, it offered $10.00 for best letters

on "Is Dr. Henry Right?" or "Is Dr. Henry Wrong?"—
as if my rightness or wrongness were the important issue.
Across these years I have had good fellowship with the
gifted scholar who then said "Nein!," the more so since
he later changed his mind.

In *Uneasy Conscience* I pleaded with American fundamentalism to come out of the woods and into the world with
its proclamation of the whole counsel of God. In *Christian
Personal Ethics* I shaped the structure of an evangelical case
for revealed morality and set it in the context of the world
of philosophical thought on the premise that Christ alone
is the King of truth. It was then my intention to complete
Christian Social Ethics in three volumes on which I had
already spent a great deal of time—"Christianity and the
Crisis in Marriage and the Home," "Christianity and the
Crisis in Labor and Economics," and "Christianity and the
Crisis in the State and Culture." But my assumption in 1956
of the editorship of *Christianity Today* (for a year only,
as I then thought) has erased the opportunity for sustained
creative writing necessary to its completion. Meanwhile the
modern social crisis has steadily worsened and a religio-
moral assessment needs desperately to be made from an
evangelical point of view.

In *Aspects of Christian Social Ethics* I have indicated
some of the governing principles of such an assessment.
Never has it seemed as important as now to stress some
things—negatively, that the institutional Church has no
divine mandate, authority or competence to endorse political
parties, legislative programs or particular candidates; and
positively, that individual Christians have a duty to be
active in public affairs to the limit of their competence, and
that the clergy are obliged to preach the divinely revealed
principles of morality and the only saving Gospel. Whatever
a Christian does in the world he must do as a matter of

spiritual obedience; his role in the world does not impose a second task independent of his evangelical mission, but is another way of affirming Christ as Saviour and Lord.

More is required of those to whom much is given; but it is required of all that they make sure the word they hear and obey is that of the self-revealed God, and not that of self-appointed arbiters of human destiny. Whose strong voice will be heard in the wildernesses of modernity, gathering into a single universe of discourse the realities of logos and life and light and law and love? As you traverse neglected paths and untried ways to reach the modern man you may seem for a time a strange breed of evangelical even to devout friends. But when they see no evidence of harm coming to your witness, when they realize that a wider impact for Christ is being registered on the world, when they recognize that you have led the way to new frontiers while others waited and doubted, they will honor you. Under God they will cheer your devout sense of evangelical vocation—whether in outer space, or in international law, or in national politics, or in public teaching, or at missionary outposts that still demand a martyr-spirit, or in a pulpit that ministers faithfully to men whose world keeps falling apart as well as to men struggling to put it together.

Perhaps, despite all that I have said, somebody here is looking for a bomb shelter in which to propagate the evangelical faith. If so, let me propose a change on your reading list: retire your Bible to the Smithsonian Institute and get a copy of the Dead Sea Scrolls instead. The Essene caves are waiting for you. You won't have to worry about the world outside. You won't even have to worry about neo-evangelicals. You won't have to worry about anything. And in A.D. 4000 some roving archaeologists from Mars may discover in those Judean hills that, during the great crisis of the twentieth century, Saint Kilroy slept here.

Chapter IV

EVANGELICALS IN THE SOCIAL STRUGGLE

Evangelical Christianity today confronts a "new theology," a "new evangelism," and a "new morality," each notably lacking in Biblical content. A "new social ethics" has also emerged, and some ecumenical leaders mainly interested in politico-economic issues speak hopefully of a "new breed of evangelical" in this realm of activity. The red carpet rolls out when even a few evangelicals march at Selma, when they unite in organized picket protests and public demonstrations, when they join ecclesiastical pressure blocs on Capitol Hill or at the White House, or when they engineer resolutions on legislative matters through annual church meetings.

Since most evangelical churchmen traditionally have not mobilized their social concern in this way, non-evangelical sociologists are delighted over any and every such sign of apparent enlightenment. Moreover, they propagandize such church techniques as authentically Christian, and misrepresent evangelical nonparticipation as proof of social indifference in conservative Christian circles and as a lack of compassion. This favorite device of propagandists is effective among some evangelicals who desire to protect their genuine devotion to social concern from public mis-

51

interpretation. The claim that evangelicals as a whole are socially impotent, moreover, diverts attention from the long-range goals of social extremists by concentrating attention on existential involvement on an emergency basis.

That Christians are citizens of two worlds, that a divine mandate enjoins their preaching of the Gospel and their promotion of social justice, that the lordship of Christ over all of life involves sociocultural obligations, that Christians bear a political responsibility, are historic evangelical emphases. Evangelicals regard government and jurisprudence as strategic realms of vocational service to humanity. They stress that government exists for the sake of all citizens, not simply for certain favored groups, and that a just or good society preserves for all citizens equal rights before the law. This emphasis has equally critical implications for a society that seeks special privilege for one race above another and for any church that seeks partisan and sectarian benefits from government.

The heritage of evangelical Christianity includes both Jesus' Sermon on the Mount and His delineation of the Good Samaritan, and Paul's account of civil government as an agent of justice. Evangelical Christians recognized the moral claim of these scriptural elements long before Protestant liberalism distorted them into a rationalistic politico-economic perspective. The Evangelical Revival in eighteenth- and nineteenth-century Britain attested the devotion of believers, not only to the observance of public statutes, but also to the vigorous promotion of just laws. William Wilberforce (1754-1833) headed the movement in Parliament that led in 1807 to the abolition of slavery in the British Empire. As a result of his own conversion, the seventh Earl of Shaftesbury (1801-1880) led great reform programs, including child-labor laws. The Evangelical Revival placed evangelicals in the forefront of humanitarian concerns, not only for an end to the slave trade, but also for child labor laws, prison reforms, improved factory labor conditions, and much else in the sphere of social justice. It was evangelical social concern, in fact, that preserved the shape of Anglo-Saxon society from tragic revolutionary onslaught.

An eminent church historian writes: "No branch indeed of the Western Church can be refused the honor of having assisted in the progress of humane ideas, and non-Christians have participated largely in the work of diffusing the modern spirit of kindness; but the credit of the inception of the movement belongs without doubt to that form of Protestantism which is distinguished by the importance it attaches to the doctrine of the Atonement. . . . History shows that the thought of Christ on the Cross has been more potent than anything else in arousing a compassion for suffering and indignation at injustice. . . . The later Evangelicalism, which saw in the death of Christ the means of free salvation for fallen humanity, caused its adherents to take the front rank as champions of the weak. . . . Prison reform, the prohibition of the slave trade, the abolition of slavery, the Factory Acts, the protection of children, the crusade against cruelty to animals, are all the outcome of the great Evangelical Revival of the eighteenth century. The humanitarian tendencies of the nineteenth century, which, it is but just to admit, all Christian communities have fostered, and which non-Christian philanthropists have vied with them in encouraging, are among the greatest triumphs of the power and influence of Christ" (F. J. Foakes-Jackson, "Christ in the Church: The Testimony of History," in H. B. Swete, *Cambridge Theological Essays,* New York, 1905, pp. 512-14).

For two generations liberal social ethics has been markedly influential in American public life in the areas of education, government, and labor. Liberal ecclesiastical reformers have only themselves to blame for the present lack of fixed governing principles in public policy, and for the declining spiritual influence of their churches in the private sector of national life. One theologian addicted to a radically secular version of Christianity—Professor William Hamilton of Colgate-Rochester Divinity School—tells us candidly that "we are well into the opening phase of the breakdown of organized religion in American life, well beyond the time when ecumenical dialogue or denominational mergers can be expected to arrest the breakdown" *(The Christian Scholar,* Spring, 1965).

Professor Hamilton fails to recognize, however, that the modernist dilution of historic Christian theology was largely responsible for compromising the message and power of institutional Christianity. In no century of recent history have public structures been so directly influenced by American churchmen as they are in our time through the pressures of liberal social thought. Churchmen have increasingly manipulated the machinery of ecumenical Christianity in support of socio-economic objectives, including specific legislative proposals. Not even the breakdown of the League of Nations or the deformation of the United Nations, each endorsed as the world's best hope for peace, has encouraged "second thoughts" about the efficacy or legitimacy of the nature of their social activity.

This does not mean that evangelical Christians have reason to boast about social alertness on the explosive frontiers of public life. They were undeniably concerned with personal behavior in public social life, and with responsible community involvement in keeping with the standards and vocations of believers. To their further credit they realized that not an ethic of grace but rather an ethic of justice should govern social structures (including international relations, national government, and legal institutions generally). But evangelical Christians elaborated no Bible-based ethic impinging on the basis, method, and function of social structures and groups such as the state, labor movements and business corporations, minorities, and so on.

If excuses for neglect are in order, this may be the right place to note them. Evangelicals could plead, of course, that the "social gospeler's" neglect of God's good news of salvation for sinners imposed upon conservative Christianity the burden of Biblical evangelism and missions throughout a perishing world—a staggering task indeed. Evangelical capability was decimated by liberal control of denominations, schools, and other ecclesiastical resources. But evangelical withdrawal from the arena of public life came mainly in reaction to the Protestant liberal attempts to achieve the Kingdom of God on earth through political and economic changes. The modernists so excluded supernatural redemptive facets of the Christian faith and so modified the proper content of the Christian ethic that, as evangelicals saw it, they had altered the very nature and mission of the Church. Evangelical Christianity reacted against the liberal Protestant concentration of effort in this area of concern by non-involvement, and this withdrawal yielded the field to the speculative theories of liberal churchmen and largely deprived evangelicals of an ethical witness in the mainstream of public life.

Precisely what is objectionable in liberal social ethics from the evangelical viewpoint? This is no small matter, for criticism extends to presuppositions, methods, and goals.

The theological presuppositions of liberal social ethics are hostile to Biblical theology. A generation ago the "social gospel" theologians deleted the wrath of God and dissolved His righteousness into benevolence or love; today the revolt has been extended. Dialectical and existential moralists surrender the objective being of God, while secular theologians disown His transcendence and, for that matter, His relevance as well. What passes for Christian social ethics in such circles dispenses with the supernatural essence of the Christian religion as foreign to problems of social justice and public righteousness. Evangelicals who insist on obedience to divinely revealed precepts, and who hold that redeemed men alone can truly fulfill the will of God and that only men of good will can enlarge the boundaries of God's Kingdom, are caricatured as "rationalists," despite the fact that Scripture specifically associates Jesus' mission with an era of good will on earth. Yet while existentialists reject the absolutes of a transcendent morality for an absolute of their own decision, thereby making each person his own church, and reject an ethics based on principles because they consider it impossible to achieve moral obedience by decree, they nonetheless agitate for laws to compel others to act in a predictable, principled way.

It may seem pedantic, if not picayune, in a secular society so perilously near doom, to surround the moral demand for *agape* with a complex of theological distinctions. After all, is not *agape* itself the central Christian moral motif? But the reply is simple: "*agape*" stripped of supernatural elements is no longer Biblical *agape*. For Biblical *agape* is first and foremost the love of God. Biblical *agape* is nowhere simply a matter of humanistic charity toward one's neighbors. "You shall love the Lord, your God, with all your heart, and with all your soul, and with all your mind, and your neighbor as yourself"—love them, as a well-phrased prayer reiterates, "with a pure heart, fervently." Although just laws are desirable and imperative, law has the power only of outward restraint; it lacks power to ensure outward obedience and inner conformity to its command. In the absence of moral men—of men willing to do the good—no body of law, however just, can ensure a good society. Authentic Christian ethics concerns what is done through a desire to do God's will, in obedience to His command; this is made possible only by spiritual regeneration. No other motivation can counter the selfish drives that haunt the noblest of unredeemed men and correct the faulty vision of an unredeemed society.

The current existential appeal for everyman's "identification with others" naïvely presupposes that the "identifiers" are morally equipped with motivations unthwarted by selfishness. But universal love, even in diluted forms, is a requirement that far exceeds the capacity of unregenerate men; for a Jew to have loved Hitler must have posed a problem not unlike that involved in a Selma marcher's love for the governor of Alabama, or a Birmingham demonstrator's affection for the local sheriff. The modern devotion to mankind *in place of* God, on the premise of "the infinite worth of the individual," indicates the inability of some Western intellectuals to assimilate the basic lessons of recent history. They blandly overlook the power of evil in human nature and man's limitations in coping with it—witness not only the patent egoism of individuals and social collectivities and the barbarism of the dictators, but also the tragic fact of two world wars at the pinnacle of Western scientific development and the unresolved threat of imminent universal destruction. As George F. Thomas says, "man is neither infinite nor perfect, and his ideal ends are worthy of devotion only insofar as they are subordinated to the purpose of One who is both" (*Religious Philosophies of the West,* New York, Charles Scribner's Sons, 1965, p. 351).

The evangelical Christian mobilizes for social action in the spiritual context of transcendent justice, supernatural law, revealed principles, concern for God's will in human affairs, and love of God and man. Against ecclesiastical "young Turks" who propagandize the notion that social concerns cannot be expressed within the inherited theology, the evangelical contends that insofar as social concerns are authentically Biblical, they can be adequately expressed and fulfilled only within scriptural theology. What the evangelical does in the social order, as in every other realm of life, he does as a matter of principled spiritual obedience to the Lord of life.

It is, moreover, a gross underestimation of differences in social action between evangelicals and non-evangelicals to imply that, beyond motivation, they agree wholly on goals and differ only in method. The liberal Protestant identification of Christian love with pacifism, then with socialism, even with Communism by some modernists in the recent past, is too fresh a memory to allow one to blunder into the notion that the Bible sanctions whatever social goals the liberal moralists endorse. Even the Communist hostility toward supernatural religion as an unscientific myth has moderated into tactical tolerance of religion as useful for promoting a social consciousness agreeable to the Soviet politico-economic ideology. Repudiation of private property, of the profit motive, and of inequality of wealth, and other Marxist ideals have been arbitrarily promoted by liberal social reformers in supposed devotion to the Biblical vision of the Kingdom of God. Even their emphasis on equal rights has cheaply surrendered property rights as a fundamental human right, and also man's right to work apart from compulsory union membership.

Whenever the Church advances a political ideology or promotes partisan legislation, its ecclesiastical leaders are soon forced into the position of impugning the integrity of influential Christians who sincerely dissent from the official views. It should surprise nobody, therefore, that as the National Council of Churches comes under increasing fire, its spokesmen tend to demean critics of its political commitments as reactionary advocates of arrogant nationalism and of social, economic, and racial privilege.

Not a few goals approved by modern social theorists are wholly desirable, and evangelical differences in such cases concern the means of achieving these ends. Elimination of poverty, opportunity for employment, racial equality, and many other goals that stand at the heart of contemporary social agitation are not only acceptable but highly desirable. Evangelicals are not indifferent to the desirability of such objectives even if liberal social ethics mistakenly conceives the Kingdom of God as basically a politico-economic phenomenon and tends to dilute redemptive spiritual forces into sociological ingredients. In fact, as evangelicals see it, such features of social life are essential to a just and good society.

Evangelicals no less than liberals recognize social justice as an authentic Christian concern, despite serious differences over definition and content. If evangelicals came to stress evangelism above social concern, it was because of liberalism's skepticism over supernatural redemptive dynamisms and its pursuit of the Kingdom of God by sociological techniques only. Hence a sharp and costly disjunction arose, whereby many evangelicals made the mistake of relying on evangelism alone to preserve world order and many liberals made the mistake of relying wholly on socio-political action to solve world problems.

It would be naïve to argue from this, however, that liberals and evangelicals need each other for complementary emphases. Over and above differences of motivation and of goals stand the differences between evangelical and liberal ethics in respect to methodology. Most evangelicals reject outright the liberal methodology of social reform, in which more and more liberals call for a "new evangelism" that substitutes sociological for spiritual concerns. Just as in his theological view of God the liberal dissolves righteousness

into love, so in the political order he dilutes social justice
into compassion. This kind of merger not only destroys the
Biblical view of God on the one hand but also produces
the welfare state on the other. This confounding of justice
and love confuses what God expects of government with
what He expects of the Church, and makes the state an
instrument for legislating partisan and sectarian ideals upon
society. Ideally the purpose of the state is to preserve justice,
not to implement benevolence; ideally, the purpose of the
Church is to preach the Gospel and to manifest unmerited,
compassionate love.

Many sociologists and political scientists dislike this way
of stating the case. But it is noteworthy that these particular
disciplines are especially barren of evangelical perspectives;
they tend to be theologically illiterate in respect both to
eschatology and to a basic theology of justice. Current
proposals to detach the Gospel from "right-wing" social
reaction and current pleas for "political compassion" are
rooted in leftist political ideology more often than in an
authentic spiritual view of the role of government.

But in the present explosive era of history the problem
of acting on an acceptable methodology is an urgent one
for evangelicals. It is one thing to deplore ministerial
marches and picket lines and well-publicized public pressures; but if evangelical conscience is to be a remedial and
transforming social force, then evangelical convictions require articulate mobilization on their own account.

Despite the present confusion caused by ecclesiastical
intervention in political affairs, evangelicals have something
socially relevant to say to both the secular man and the
church man. The Christian has social duties not simply as
a Christian but as a man, and his sanctification therein
does not come about automatically without pulpit instruc-
tion in sound scriptural principles. Evangelicals as a people

view themselves as bound to the Word of God; for this reason they consider themselves a spiritual people with a divine message for themselves and for others in regard to social action. Evangelicals acknowledge a divine call to identify themselves with others—not with social customs or social vices or social discontents, but rather with persons in their survival needs: physical and moral and spiritual. These survival needs include material help in destitution, social justice, and the redemption that is in Christ Jesus.

Surely evangelical Christianity has more to offer mankind than its unique message of salvation, even if that is its highest and holiest mission. While it rightly chides the liberal for regarding the world as a unity (rather than divided into unregenerate and regenerate), it also has a message for all men as members of one society. The Christian is not, by his church identification, isolated from humanity, or from involvement in the political and economic orders. Not only is he called to identify himself with society: he *is* identified, by the very fact of his humanity, and as a Christian he bears a double responsibility in relation to the social needs and goals of mankind. Social justice is a need of the individual, whose dignity as a person is at stake, and of society and culture, which soon collapse without it.

The evangelical knows that spiritual regeneration restores men to moral earnestness; but he also knows the moral presuppositions of a virile society, and he is obligated to proclaim the "whole counsel" of God. He may have no message for society that insures unrepentant mankind against final doom—nor even against catastrophic destruction in our own time, while its leaders insist upon arbitrary human authority at the expense of the lordship of Jesus Christ. But he can and ought to use every platform of social involvement to promulgate the revealed moral principles that sustain a healthy society and that indict an unhealthy one. More than this, the evangelical Christian should be represented, in his personal convictions, on the frontiers of government and in the corporate processes of society. Convinced that the cooperation of godly men in the social and collective order can be decisively influential, he should be concerned about relations between nations and about minority rights. There is no reason at all why evangelical Christians should not engage energetically in projecting social structures that promote the interests of justice in every public realm; in fact, they have every legitimate sanction for social involvement.

Of course the Church is to be ruled distinctively by an ethic of grace. But the Church is also in a world that is to be ruled by justice, an ethic of justice that does not *per se* require regenerate social structures. In this context, a positive ethic and corrective principles enunciated on the broad world scene by regenerate believers who are engaged in the social struggle can have decisive influence. Such an ethic will include (1) the Church's faithful exposition of divinely revealed standards of human justice as the only basis for a stable society and as the criteria by which the world will be finally judged; and (2) the Christian's energetic promotion and support of just laws as the formal hallmark of a good society. When Christian believers become thus involved in the struggle for justice, the world may recognize in a new way the presence of regenerate realities; noting the community of twice-born men that sees the restoration of sinners to fellowship with God and to holiness as the aim of the Gospel, the world may even recognize the validity of regenerate structures through their moral impact.

Any Christian engaged in the pursuit of social justice is painfully aware that, in a tragic world of fallen men, government decisions often involve a choice between greater and lesser evils rather than between absolutes of good and evil, and that only the Church of Christ can witness to a manifestation of absolute good in history. He will, however, avoid both the liberal error of "absolutizing relatives," as if these were identical with the will of God, and also the fundamentalist temptation to consider any gain short of the absolute ideal in history as worthless or unworthy.

But evangelicals must not perpetuate the liberal Protestant failure to distinguish between the social concerns of *law* and the social concern of *gospel*. In law and justice—that is, the province of government—all men are obliged to support man's God-given rights as universally due to human beings whatever their race, color, or creed. The evangelical knows that no improvement can be made on a government that assures every man his rights, and that limits the freedom of citizens where and when it intrudes upon the rights of others. Evangelicals do not view government as an instrument of benevolence or compassion, since love is preferential and shows favor or partiality. Constantly pressing the question, "Don't you care?," liberals enlist support for legislating programs of benevolence. Such an appeal to "compassion" in support of legislative programs commits a twofold error, however: it diverts government from an ideal preservation of equal human rights before the law, and it shifts to the state a responsibility for compassion or benevolence that belongs properly to the Church. By concentrating on government to achieve the goals of both state and Church in a "benevolent partnership," liberalism reflects a reliance on political techniques in society to the neglect of the redemptive dynamisms inherent in Christianity. This reliance on political techniques to achieve ecclesiastical objectives means the loss of a genuine supernatural grounding of ethical concerns, the loss of the Church as Church in society, the loss of the redemptive evangel to secular solvents of social malformity, and the loss of evangelical loyalties in the congregation.

What distinguishes evangelical Christianity is its refusal to impose sectarian obligations upon government, upon government which then employs compulsion to enforce a program of benevolence that individual citizens might or might not approve. Even if they did approve, they might consider the provision of such benevolences moral only if performed voluntarily; or they might consider it immoral to use taxation to compel others to do what they do not think to be right. While liberals justify their breaking of laws that appear unjust on the grounds of sensitivity to conscience, they nonetheless promote other laws that some persons regard as preferential and unjust.

To the evangelical Christian, the best alternative to the "welfare" state is the just state, and the best alternative to political demonstrations is civil obedience. The evangelical champions and strives for just legislation, and for obedience to law and respect for judicial process rather than for directly coerced action. The evangelical sponsors a principled ethic whose course is determined by divinely revealed moral principles. Much of contemporary liberal social action is not a matter of obeying laws; rather, it is a case of everyone's being on his existential own. Dialectical-existential ethics cannot indicate in advance what the moral agent ought to do, and looks upon any structured objective ethics as mere rationalism.

The evangelical holds that all persons are divinely obligated by the Scriptures to love their neighbors. While progress has been slow in the area of race tensions, nonetheless there has been progress. Yet even evangelical believers fall short of their highest moral aspirations, and laws are necessary to hold just social standards before Christians and non-Christians alike. All citizens should strive to replace discriminatory laws by non-discriminatory laws. The evangelical recognizes, however, that without public enthusiasm only moral earnestness vouchsafed by spiritual conviction and renewal assures the necessary devotion to right that guarantees social fulfillment. While the glory of ancient Rome was its genius for universal law, through its lack of heart for righteousness the Roman Empire sank into oblivion. The problem of racial discrimination can be permanently met only by Christian behavior that faces up to the ugliness of bias, the evils of immorality and delinquency, and the whole complex of problems that surrounds race feeling. The predilection for public issues over personal holiness in liberal social ethics is all the more disconcerting in view of this fact. Although liberal churchmen will throw their energies behind a public health program, they tend to remain silent about many of the personal vices; such concerns are left to the "purity nuts."

The history of Christian mission in the world makes it clear that evangelicals were interested in education, hospitals, care for the aged, and many current social concerns long before modern secular theory was ever born. Evangelicals were active in social work not only in the slums of America but also on distant mission fields a full century before the rise of modern welfare programs. To this day, rescue missions all across the land reflect a long-standing inner-city missionary concern for people in material and spiritual poverty. Evangelicals have not been as active as they need to be in the social arena; on the other hand, they have been far more active than they are sometimes said to have been.

The weakness of public demonstration as the approved means of Christian social action is its limitation and externalization of Christian concern. It is arbitrary to imply that only those who demonstrate at a given point manifest authentic social concern. Moreover, since local demonstrations gain national significance through radio and television, the implications of massive civil disobedience are the more distressing. Ecclesiastical demonstrators who never persuade observers to become disciples of Jesus Christ ought to ask how effectively Christian is such amorphous "witness by demonstration." The motivations for demonstrating are internal, and apart from verbal interpretation might equally well be sub-Christian, non-Christian, or anti-Christian. As a matter of fact, Jews and humanists resent a Christian interpretation of their demonstrating.

If authentic social concern demanded the ecumenical chartering of planes to officially designated out-of-town points, it would require a large expense account to enable everybody to travel to somebody else's home town "to identify." If every supporter of an item of disputed legislation had to march to Capitol Hill, if every Christian citizen had to put in a personal appearance to let legislators know what laws he thought God specially wanted, what would tourist-jammed Washington be like then? If the representative role of congressmen were superseded by the group pressures of ministers, the whole machinery of American government would soon collapse. The question remains, moreover: Whose conscience answers for whom? These clergy are received by congressmen, not on the premise that they speak only for themselves, but as voices for their churches. No one disputes a clergyman's right as an individual to picket or demonstrate anywhere he wishes (the right of conscience is a Protestant principle). It is unlikely, however, that pastors can wholly detach themselves from responsibilities to their congregations. When prominent churchmen parade as Reverend Church, moreover, they are simply encouraging future counter-demonstrations at 475 Riverside Drive or at denominational headquarters.

What many socially sensitive ministers especially deplore is the implication left by the well-publicized minority of marchers that nonmarchers are lacking or inferior in social concern. "I don't mind another minister's marching if he must relieve his conscience that way," said one Washington minister, "but I don't see why my social concern—never before questioned—should now be in doubt because I didn't engage in this form of exhibitionism." In Copenhagen, when Evangelist Billy Graham opened his crusade, a heckler interrupted him with the cry: "Why didn't you march in Selma?" But Graham had been integrating meetings in the South long before some of the marchers had become existentialized and, moreover, had done so in the context of Biblical Christianity. It is a neat propaganda device to imply that evangelical social concern is immobile because it does not conform to liberal methods—it merely proves that political propagandism is a technique in which liberal ecclesiastical leaders have become adept. In some ecclesiastical circles, the defense of this one controversial method of action has apparently justified the repudiation of all theological grounds of social concern.

When evangelicals manifest social concern, they do so first by proclaiming the supernatural revelation of God and the historical resurrection of Jesus Christ. Thus they emphasize the transcendent basis of justice and the divine basis of the Gospel. They declare both the standards by which Almighty God will judge the human race and the redemption from sin unto holiness that is to be found in Jesus Christ. They affirm God's institution of civil government to preserve justice and order, and the Church as a spiritual fellowship of redeemed men who esteem their neighbors in holy love and dedicate themselves to social righteousness.

The evangelical Christian's social concern is first directed toward the family as the basic unit of society. He finds a hollow ring in the social passion for "one world" that simultaneously lacks indignation over divorce, infidelity, and vagrancy in the home. Because liberalism fails to see society as a macrocosm of the family, it is bankrupt to build a new society. Liberalism changes ideological loyalties and social perspectives every generation; evangelical Christianity treasures the family bound to the changeless will of God and to the apostolic faith. Hence evangelical Christianity regards the Sunday school, the prayer meeting, and the family in the church as a cohesive social unit that reflects in miniature the ideal social order.

No new era of brotherliness and peace is likely to emerge in the absence of a new race of men. Evangelicals consider alliances of nations uncommitted to transcendent justice to be as futile a foundation for future mutuality as premarital promiscuity. As evangelical Christians see it, the vision of One World or of United Nations that is built on geographical representation rather than on principial agreement is as socially unpromising as is a lawless home that neglects the commandments of God. Walter Lippman has somewhere said: "We ourselves were so sure that at long last a generation had arisen, keen and eager to put this disorderly earth to right . . . and fit to do it . . . We meant so well, we tried so hard, and look what we have made of it. We can only muddle into muddle. What is required is a new kind of man."

Evangelical Christianity finds the most natural avenue for social witness beyond the family circle in the world of work when it is viewed as a divine calling. How sadly liberal Christianity, during its past-generation domination of ecclesiastical life, has failed in the organized church's social witness is nowhere more apparent than here. Almost all political leaders of the race-torn states are church members; Alabama's Governor Wallace belongs to the Methodist Church, which is in the forefront of liberal social action programs.

Almost all congressmen are church members. Either the religious social activists have failed miserably in inspiring churchmen in political life to view their vocations as avenues for the advancement of socal justice, or an elite ecclesiastical cadre is pressuring leaders to conform their political judgments to the partisan preferences of a special bloc of churchmen—or perhaps both are true. Since everyone lives in a world of labor and economics, evangelical Christianity emphasizes that man's work is a divinely appointed realm in which man is to glorify God and invest his talents for the good of his fellows; it is not only a means of livelihood but also an avenue of service.

This concept of divine vocation, of work as a calling, has all but vanished from the work-a-day world at the very time in modern history when liberal social action commissions have conspired with the labor unions in their skyrocketing material benefits. Meanwhile evangelical Protestants have organized a Christian Medical Society, Christian Business Men's Committee, Christian Professional Women's Club, Christian Law Society, Christian Teachers' Association, Officers Christian Union in the Armed Forces—even a Christian Labor Union—in order to emphasize the spiritual responsibilities of vocation. It must be conceded that many of these Christian organizations serve mainly an evangelistic role, or one of vocational fellowship; only a beginning has been made in the equally urgent task of shaping an ethic for the social structures in which these groups operate. Beyond fulfilling person-to-person Christian opportunities, such agencies have an opportunity to supply guidance to both Christian and non-Christian on what is implied in a specified social order in the way of justice.

Evangelical Christians consider this recognition of the priestly nature of daily work to be more basic to social renewal than is a reshuflle of economic features that locates the fundamental flaws of society in man's environment rather than in man himself and his works. The importance of just laws is not in dispute, since civil government is divinely designed as a coercive force to restrain evil, preserve order, and promote justice in a fallen and sinful society. Because there is no assurance that all men will repent and seek the will of God, and because even Christian believers must contend with the remnants of sin, just laws are indispensable in human history, and God's common grace in the lives of men everywhere matches conscience with law in the interest of social preservation. But evangelical Christianity recognizes that a good society turns upon the presence of good men—of regenerated sinners whose minds and hearts are effectively bound to the revealed will of God—and upon their ability under God to influence humanity to aspire to enduring values.

Although society at large has seldom been overwhelmed by the Church's proclaiming the Gospel from the pulpit, the obedient fulfillment of the Great Commission has called new disciples one by one into the circle of regenerate humanity. The voice of the Church in society has been conspicuously weaker whenever the pulpit of proclamation has been forsaken for mass pressures upon the public through the adoption of resolutions, the promotion of legislation, and the organization of demonstrations. Whenever the institutional church seeks public influence by mounting a socio-political platform, she raises more fundamental doubts about the authenticity and uniqueness of the Church than about the social aberrations against which she protests.

To evangelical Christianity, history at its best is the lengthened shadow of influential men, not the compulsive grip of impersonal environmental forces. A change of environmental forces will not transform bad men into good men—let alone into a good society. But transformed men will rise above a bad environment and will not long be lacking in a determination to alter it.

At the present time, involvement in the race problem is the crucial test of devotion to social justice. Of the evangelical Christian's love for men of all races the long-standing missionary effort leaves no doubt; from Adoniram Judson and David Livingstone to Hudson Taylor and Paul Carlson, the story is one of evangelical sacrifice of creature comforts, even of life itself, that men of every land and color might share the blessings of redemption. In mid-twentieth-century America, humanism and liberalism and evangelicalism alike were slow to protest political discrimination against the Negro, although evangelical missionaries have deplored the incongruities of segregation. Regrettably, the Negro's plight became for some liberal reformers an opportunity for promoting social revolution, and for some conservative reactionaries an occasion for perpetuating segregation and discrimination. Evangelical Christianity has a burden for social renewal but no penchant for revolution or reaction. Because it champions the redemptive realities inherent in the Christian religion, evangelical Christianity will vindicate the judgment that the Negro is not only politically an equal but also spiritually a brother.

A new breed of evangelical? Yes, indeed! But not because evangelicals are switching from proclamation of the good tidings to pronouncements, picketing, and politicking as sacred means of legislating Christian sentiment on earth. Rather, evangelicals are a new breed because redemptive religion seeks first and foremost a new race of men, new creatures in Christ. Whenever Christians lose that motivation, they surrender more than their New Testament distinctiveness; they forfeit the New Testament evangel as well.

In summary, evangelicals face the social predicament today with four controlling convictions:

1. The Christian Church's distinctive dynamic for social transformation is personal regeneration by the Holy Spirit, and the proclamation of this divine offer of redemption is the Church's prime task.

In the twentieth century the ecumenical movement has failed most conspicuously in its mission to the world by relying on political and sociological forces, and by neglecting spiritual dynamisms.

2. While the corporate or institutional church has no divine mandate, jurisdiction, or special competence for approving legislative proposals or political parties and persons, the pulpit is responsible for proclaiming divinely revealed principles of social justice as a part of the whole counsel of God.

3. The most natural transition from private to social action occurs in the world of daily work, in view of the Christian's need to consecrate his labor to the glory of God and to the service of mankind.

4. As citizens of two worlds, individual church members have the sacred duty to extend God's purpose of redemption through the Church, and also to extend God's purpose of justice and order through civil government. Christians are to distinguish themselves by civil obedience except where this conflicts with the commandments of God, and are to use every political opportunity to support and promote just laws, to protest social injustice, and to serve their fellow men.

Chapter V

WHAT IS CHRISTIANITY?

Every scholar knows that Christianity has been more variously defined in our century than at any other time in the long history of Western thought. Today intellectual formulations run the wide range from Karl Barth's *Church Dogmatics* to Paul Tillich's *Systematic Theology*, just as a generation ago they covered the vast distance between J. Gresham Machen's *The Origin of Paul's Religion* and Shailer Matthews' *The Faith of Modernism* and Wieman and Meland's *Is There a God?*, and in the forepart of this century spanned the great gulf between James Orr's *The Christian View of God and the World* and Adolf Harnack's *What Is Christianity?* In such conflicting representations of the Christian religion the disunity of the Christian Church in recent times finds some of its deepest roots.

In a moment of unecumenical candor, *The Christian Century* noted editorially on January 3, 1924, that "the differences between Fundamentalism [which was the *Century's* 'color word' for biblical theism] and modernism . . . are foundation differences, structural differences, amounting in their radical dissimilarity almost to the difference between two distinct religions" (p. 159). With equal frankness Dr. Samuel C. Craig, long editor of *The Presbyterian,*

stated in 1946 that his book *Christianity Rightly So Called*
aimed to distinguish "between Christianity and its counter-
feits" in the face of conceptions of Christianity so radically
different that if any of them is true, many of them must
necessarily be false.

The question "What is Christianity?" must be answered
normatively in terms of the ideal, and not descriptively in
terms of the present historical situation, for taken descriptively, Christianity now bears such a multitude of meanings
as virtually to rob the term of any fixed content whatever
in general parlance. The term is used not only to designate
the redemptive supernaturalism of the Bible (in the diver-
gent expositions of Eastern Orthodoxy, Roman Catholicism
and Protestantism) but also a vast variety of cults from
Mormonism to Christian Science. It is claimed by champions of a personal ethics broadly imitative of Jesus as a
man, or of a social ethics of sacrificial good will and
altruistic devotion to the community, and by such a gamut
of speculative philosophies that some critics consider Christianity no less difficult to define than to believe.

How then are we to characterize that "pure religion" of
which the apostle James wrote? What is the essence of
Christianity?

First of all, Christianity is an historical religion; it arose
at a given juncture of history in a specific historical climate.
As Professor Machen has rightly pointed out, then, Christianity is "subject to historical investigation . . . As an historical phenomenon it must be investigated on the basis of
evidence . . . What Christianity is can be determined only
by an examination of the beginnings of Christianity" (J.
Gresham Machen, *Christianity and Liberalism;* Grand
Rapids, Michigan: Wm. B. Eerdmans Publishing Company, 1946, p. 19).

An appeal to the historical records is precisely how scholarship must determine the content of any historical religion. Conceivably, Christianity may now have to be abandoned, and displaced by another religion, but it ought to be expounded on its own presuppositions and tested by appropriate criteria. This approach preserves those original features of a record which a modern exponent might for personal reasons be tempted to ignore or to delete. So, for example, in an essay on "What Is the Christian Religion?," Yale theologian D. C. Macintosh argued that redemption by the blood of Christ as a sacrifice for sin is "not only not essential to Christianity because contrary to reason, but moreover essentially unchristian because opposed to the principles of sound morality" (Douglas Clyde Macintosh, "What is the Christian Religion?" in *Harvard Theological Review,* January, 1914). Professor Macintosh ventured to establish the essence of the Christian religion by postulating what was rationally congruous with his own presuppositions and agreeable to his own moral conceptions, and not by sound historical inquiry into the religion founded by Christ and the apostles. Such an approach arbitrarily makes one's own prejudices, rather than historical considerations, the touchstone in defining essential Christianity.

Many contemporaries consider belief in the supernatural to be rationally unjustifiable, and even morally objectionable—at least, the followers of Karl Marx and other naturalists, including "death of God" theologians so contend. But there is no doubt that the first Christians, and in fact the vast majority of Christians in all ages, have insisted on the reality and ultimacy of an invisible supernatural realm. They would contend, in fact, that it is naturalism which is rationally indefensible and morally objectionable. They would insist, moreover, that any scholar who repudiates

miraculous supernaturalism, disqualifies himself as professing champion of Christianity. Just as the Old Testament
revolves around the divine creation of the universe and
man, and around the supernatural deliverance of Israel
from Egypt, so the New Testament revolves about the
miraculous incarnation of God in Jesus Christ and about
His supernatural resurrection from the dead. Christianity
presupposes belief in God as a supernatural reality, belief
in miracles as His supernatural acts, and belief in the redemptive work of the supernatural Christ.

As the term itself implies, Christianity sprang from the
historical life and work of Jesus of Nazareth, and ascribes
its continuance as well as origin to His life and work. In
His life, death and resurrection the adherents of the Christian religion recognized Jesus as the Christ of the Old
Testament promise, as the God-sent Redeemer through
whom sinful men are granted forgiveness and reconciliation
with God and restored to a new life of holiness. Even the
most radical literary form criticism now bows to the verdict
of James Denney that "Christianity never existed in the
world as a religion in which men shared the faith of Jesus,
but was from the beginning and amid all undeniable diversities a religion in which Jesus was the object of faith"
(James Denney, *Jesus and the Gospel;* New York: A. C.
Armstrong and Son, 1909, p. 12).

One of the oldest summaries of the Christian Gospel,
that of Paul, gives the authentic tradition of its inner substance as follows "For I delivered unto you first of all that
which also I received: that Christ died for our sins according to the scriptures . . . and that he hath been raised on
the third day according to the scriptures" (I Corinthians
15:3 f.). Christianity, therefore, is that scriptural religion
which is rooted in the unique and final revelation of the
Creator-Redeemer God incarnate in Jesus Christ.

The first Christians were more than profoundly impressed by the grandeur of Jesus' character; they were convinced that He culminated and fulfilled the special redemptive revelation divinely given to Israel, and believed that His unique relation to the spiritual world is such that He is to be honored as man's divine Saviour and Lord. As depicted throughout the New Testament the early Christians showed no interest in schemes of speculative philosophy, nor in mystical religious rituals, nor even in a new code of ethics. Their passion, rather, was devotion to the person of Jesus Christ as the proper object of worship and obedience. They were fully persuaded, on what seemed to them adequate historical and experiential grounds, that Jesus had risen from the dead. They not only sought and found forgiveness of sins and new spiritual life in and through Him, but as their ascended and living Redeemer permeated their lives, also experienced a sense of new direction, vitality and hope.

What the early Christians believed, what they preached, what they propagated, and what established more and more Christian churches even before the Gospels were written, was the conviction that the promised Messiah of Old Testament prophecy was none other than Jesus of Nazareth, God come in the flesh for the salvation of sinners, and that the now risen Head of the Church who triumphed over sin, death and Satan had lived a sinless life and died a vicarious death.

"The Christian essentials," writes John Dickie, "are those elements, historical and dogmatic, without which Christianity would lose in whole or in part its living power to reconcile sinful man to the all-righteous, loving God" *(International Standard Bible Encyclopedia;* Grand Rapids, Michigan: Wm. E. Eerdmans Publishing Company, 1955, Vol. I, p. 624). This statement reminds us that the Christian revelation of God and His purposes involves much more than just a few unrelated assertions about the nature and work of deity. In other words, Christianity is a religious totality, not a piece-meal commentary on unrelated facets of life and being. The Christian view of God commits one also to specific assertions about both the eternal and the temporal orders— in short, to a specific view of the universe, of man and of the final destiny of all things. Christianity is no scientific theory, nor speculative philosophy. Rather, as a consequence of special divine revelation, it stands committed to its own world view, its own interpretation of the whole of reality and existence. It refers the natural, the moral, and the historical orders to one ultimate principle of explanation, namely, to the self-revealing God who defines the content of the religion of redemption. As Gordon H. Clark remarks, "Christianity is a comprehensive view of all things; it takes the world, both material and spiritual, to be an ordered system" (Gordon H. Clark, *A Christian View of Men and Things;* Grand Rapids, Michigan: Wm. B. Eerdmans Publishing Company, 1952, p. 25).

What Christianity means by redemption is not a matter of ambiguity, but of specific declaration. As a redemptive religion it offers to fallen and sinful man salvation from the penalty, the pollution and, ultimately, the presence of sin. While the classic moral philosophers and founders of other world religions teach that man may and should achieve moral perfection by the gradual improvement of his present nature, Christianity teaches, to the contrary, that only through the atoning death of Christ and the regeneration and sanctification of the Holy Spirit is fallen man restored to fellowship with his righteous Creator and to a life of holiness. The sinner's plight is such, says the Christian religion, that he needs supernatural rescue; in the terms of Scripture, he requires nothing less than justification, regeneration and sanctification. These benefits the sinner is offered in the vicarious life and death and resurrection of Jesus Christ and in the recreative work of the Holy Spirit. Christianity emphasizes, therefore, that "the works of the flesh," that is, of the natural or unregenerate man, are so weighted with ungodly motivation, if not direction, that they cannot produce a life of moral virtue. The royal route to moral perfection, it insists, is not the gradual development of the old nature, but rather the crucifixion of the old and the birth of a new nature. "Except a man be born again," said Jesus, "he cannot see the kingdom of God" (John 3:3).

While personal faith is a condition of salvation, the ground of God's redemption of sinners is the substitutionary life and death of Christ. As Craig puts it, "The object of Christian faith has never been Christ *simpliciter* but always Christ *as crucified.* . . . A Christianity that knows nothing of Jesus as crucified for sin has no more right to call itself Christianity than has a Christianity that knows nothing of a Divine Christ. . . . The essence of Christianity has always been to its adherents the sinner's experience of reconciliation with God through the propitiatory sacrifice of Jesus Christ" (Samuel G. Craig, *Christianity Rightly So Called;* Philadelphia: Presbyterian and Reformed Publishing Company, 1946, pp. 65, 73 f). While the deity of Christ, His supernatural birth of the virgin, His sinless life, His words of grace, as well as His miracles are integral elements of the Christian religion, they are not the only important elements. Especially it is the death of Christ for sinners that comes into view when the New Testament writers speak of the astonishing *agape* of God. All major branches of the Christian Church not only recognize the Cross as the symbol of the Christian religion, but in accordance with New Testament teaching also view the death of Christ as an expiatory sacri-

fice for sin. Remarkably enough, the one event Jesus commanded His disciples to commemorate was His death for
sinners (Luke 22:19). This theme of the epistles is not
foreign to the Gospels, and is anticipated in the teaching of
Jesus Himself, and also in the Old Testament writings (cf.
Luke 24:25 ff.).

That the death of Christ propitiates the wrath of God's
righteous indignation over sin, and that God's love is
manifested supremely in the gift of the Lamb slain for
sinners, is taught throughout the New Testament. Further,
the entire Bible teaches the equal ultimacy of righteousness
and love in the nature of God. Both Old and New Testa-
ments contradict the modern theory that the love of God
dissolves the need of substitutionary and propitiatory atonement: the Old, by the sacrificial scheme which prefigured
the coming of the Redeemer, and the New, by the apostolic
teaching about Christ's completed work. The Apostle Paul
speaks of Christ as the One "whom God set forth a propitiation" (Romans 3:25) and John, usually designated as the
apostle of love, declares: "Herein is love. . . . that God
loved us, and sent His Son to be the propitiation for our
sins" (I John 4:10).

As we have noted, the aim of Biblical redemption is to
overcome the guilt, penalty and pollution of sin, and to
restore the sinner to fellowship with God and to holiness.
"It is not for nothing," reads Phillips' version of the New
Testament, "that the Spirit God gives us is called the Holy
Spirit" (I Thessalonians 4:8). God's ultimate aim in forgiving sinners is their sanctification. In other words, pardon for
sin is not the whole of salvation, but rather the prelude to
purification. The Christian religion, therefore, sets before
its adherents the goal of ethical perfection; it defines the
final destiny of the righteous as complete conformity to the
image of Christ. In stressing that God is glorified by the

fruit of good works, it expounds the good life solely in terms of obedience to the revealed will of God, who is man's Creator and Judge. The Christian religion seeks a new society under the Spirit's rule, and it locates the nucleus of that society in the regenerate church of twice-born men and women whose whole duty is to love God and to love their neighbors as themselves. As participants in the two realms of state and church, the followers of Christ are called to exemplify and promote social justice, and to exhibit and proclaim redemptive grace.

In stipulating the presuppositions that underlie the Christian religion one must acknowledge a series of theological postulates based explicitly or implicitly upon the sacred Scriptures: (1) The eternal reality of a sovereign, ethical, self-revealing God, who in His nature or essence comprehends the personal distinctions of Father, Son and Holy Spirit; (2) the creation of the universe *ex nihilo* by divine fiat, and God's providential governance of it with a view to the subsequent creation of man in the divine image for spiritual and moral fellowship; (3) man's fall into sin by voluntary disobedience, his consequent guilt and exposure of the race to punishment and corruption; (4) the prophetic promise of divine redemption through a supernatural Saviour; (5) the redemptive activity of God in special relationship to Israel and coordinate revelatory activity of God in the scriptural disclosure of His purpose; (6) the fulfillment of God's promise of a Redeemer in the divine incarnation in Jesus of Nazareth, whose atonement, resurrection and heavenly priesthood shape the faith of the Christian Church; (7) the gift of the Holy Spirit, who renews men in the moral likeness of God; (8) the Christian mission to herald the offer of salvation to the world; (9) the final consummation of all things in the personal visible return of Christ, in the vindication of righteousness when the wicked are eternally separated from the blessing and prospect of redemption, and in the complete redemption and glorification of the people of God.

Christianity, therefore, is a religion of regenerate spiritual and moral life that springs from the revelation and redemption of the one true God. That is, it consists both of redemptive truths and acts, of revealed doctrines and historical facts. The Apostles' Creed is a familiar summary of supernatural events indispensable to the religion of the Bible. If the saving events attested by Scripture are but legend, if the incarnation and resurrection of Jesus Christ are but mythology, then the whole fabric of the Christian religion falls apart. Nor is Christianity a speculative philosophy postulated to explain the nature of reality and life. Neither is it reducible to a network of eternal truths. Nor is it simply a system of divinely revealed information that satisfies intellectual curiosity about the invisible world. Christianity is a redemptive religion grounded in a series of special historical events and centering in the supernatural person and work of the living Christ. But as James Orr emphasized, the historical facts of Biblical religion "do not stand blank and dumb before us, but have a voice given to them and a meaning put into them. . . . When John declares that Jesus Christ is come in the flesh and is the Son of God, he is stating a fact, but he is nonetheless enunciating a doctrine. When Paul affirms 'Christ died for our sins according to the Scriptures,' he is proclaiming a fact, but he is at the same time giving an interpretation of it" (James Orr, *The Christian View of God and the World;* New York: Charles Scribner's Sons, n.d., p. 22). The God of the Bible does not act in history like a charade performer; He does not leave mankind to interpret as best it can the meaning and significance of His redemptive deeds. That Christ died in an historical event; that He "died for our sins" is doctrinal interpretation. It is, in fact, one of the revealed truths of Scripture foundational to the whole scheme of Christian theology, and an interpretation which stems from the teaching of Jesus Himself, who spoke not only of His impending death, but of giving His life "a ransom for many."

The historical events and the Biblical doctrines, however, do not of themselves regenerate men, for it is the Holy Spirit who kindles the believer's new life in Christ. Yet the Christian life can neither exist nor thrive without knowledge of these supernatural acts and truths; sound doctrine is considered indispensable to pure religion and the root of all good conduct. A Christianity dependent upon Biblical data must necessarily be a doctrinal Christianity that rests also upon the Biblical doctrines.

This emphasis on sound doctrine presupposes for the Biblical writers that special divine guidance which they describe as the unique spiration or inspiration of the Holy Spirit (II Timothy 3:16; II Peter 1:21). Nowhere do they imply their interpretation of the facts to be mere human reflection. So interwoven is the salvation history recorded in the Bible with its meaning or interpretation that to question the writers' trustworthiness in either their historical or theological representations would cast doubt upon both the saving deeds of God and their doctrinal significance.

In defining Christianity, Christians have always treasured the Scriptures. Early Christianity admittedly flourished before the New Testament was ever written, so it is foolish to say that the existence of Christianity depends upon the New Testament, fallible or infallible. It is Christ and the Spirit who carry the Bible, and not vice versa; the Bible is the work of God's Spirit in a sense in which the Spirit is not dependent upon Scripture. "The Holy Ghost, whom the Father shall send in my name," said Jesus, "shall teach you

all things, and bring all things to your remembrance, what-
soever I have said unto you" (John 14:26).

And so the Gospels, in which the Spirit brought Jesus'
earthly teaching to the remembrance of the evangelists
and the Epistles, in which Jesus continued to teach the
apostles by the Spirit, are both carried by and carry a
divine spiritual authority. We must never forget that before
the New Testament was written, the early Christians had
the divinely given light of the Old Testament. This Old
Testament Jesus valued as a uniquely inspired corpus of
sacred writings, and Paul characterized as "the oracles of
God." Before the written New Testament, morcover, the
early Christians had the authoritative oral teaching of the
apostles.

What would have happened to the purity and integrity
of the Christian message without authoritative writings is
seen by contrasting the post-apostolic with the apostolic
writings, and by remembering the tragic eclipse of Christianity in the Middle Ages when the Bible was all but lost.
"While it is conceivable," as Craig states, "that we *could*
have a knowledge of Christianity without the Bible, there
is little reason to think we *would* have it" (Samuel G. Craig,
op. cit., p. 224). It is unlikely that the integrity of the content
of the Christian religion would have been authentically
preserved without the authoritative norm of the written
Bible.

The case for Christian theism does not rest wholly upon
the Bible. But this does not mean that the Bible is therefore untrustworthy. It is impossible to profess the authority
of Scripture without professing also its plenary inspiration
and full trustworthiness. A conflict over Scripture soon
becomes a conflict over Christ Himself who declared that
"Scripture cannot be broken." Those who profess to honor
Christ but reject the role of Scripture dishonor His view

of religious authority. Precisely the neglect, recension or rejection of one or another element of this scriptural revelation is, in fact, what has spawned the current confusion concerning the nature of the Christian religion and has made "What is Christianity?" such a probing question.

Chapter VI

CHRIST AND HIS KINGDOM

"Thy Kingdom come. Thy will be done on earth as it is in heaven. . . . And lead us not into temptation, but deliver us from evil. For thine is the Kingdom, and the power, and the glory" (Matthew 6:10-13).

Whose is this Kingdom? *What* is this Kingdom? *When* is this Kingdom? Our majestic theme serves to anticipate these three important questions.

1. *Whose is the Kingdom?* It is God's Kingdom: "Thine is the Kingdom." It is His, who is the infinite and eternal Lord of Glory; it is His, the Holy One who inhabits the eternities; it is His, who made heaven and earth by His all-powerful word; it is His, who fashioned us in His image for obedient fellowship with Himself; it is His, who promised redemption to a doomed humanity and who came in Christ to rescue us from sin and to restore us to righteousness. It is His Kingdom.

The rulers of this world strive continually for an enduring kingdom, but the Kingdom that endures God has from eternity pledged to His only Son, Jesus Christ. Man builds earthly empires only to see them vanish into the night of oblivion. Historians tell us that twenty-one great human civilizations have already arisen and perished into the dust of this earth. Once Babylon was a world power, but it has marched off the map. Once Syria was a world power; today it is a curiosity of antiquity. Once Persia was a world power; now it is a fifth-rate empire. Once Greece, once Rome, once Great Britain—one could go on and on and on, for modern man has yet to learn the obvious lesson: not even the Soviet Union and the United States are exempt from that inexorable moral and spiritual law that dictates that "righteousness exalts a nation" and that sin is a reproach to men and the highway to destruction. Unless society squares its accounts with the God of history, America will be a terrain of terror, Washington, already a city of crime, will become Washington the burg of bloody battle, and the white stars will someday tumble from our flag.

It is Christ alone who endures as the King of history, and Christ's Kingdom alone endures from age to age. That durability is one way to tell His Kingdom from spurious kingdoms such as those made in the Soviet world, lobbied in the Free World, and buried every other generation. It is Christ who finally will deliver up His Kingdom to the Father (1 Corinthians 15:24), and in that great and awesome day all the works of the other would-be dictators of human destiny will be wholly undone. In anticipating our Lord's eternal reign, the Book of Revelation exclaims: "Now is come salvation and strength, and the Kingdom of our God, and the power of his Christ . . ." (12:10)

The fact that this Kingdom is both God's and Christ's means that we are really speaking not of two Kingdoms, but of one and the same Kingdom. Some emphatically distinguish Kingdom and Church, Kingdom and Gospel, as if these were quite contrastable realities, as if the Kingdom of God could prosper where the Gospel of God and the grace of Christ are wholly unknown. But Kingdom service is ideally the regenerate service of Christ and the fulfillment of one's calling in Christ.

There is another error. The old liberal theology still subordinates the person of Jesus to the Kingdom-idea. It locates the secret of the Kingdom in Jesus' work and teaching, not in His person. The Kingdom is then defined as a life of humanitarian idealism. Gone is the supernatural Jesus, the supernatural atonement, and supernatural regeneration. To preserve this liberal dilution, John's Gospel was long misrepresented as standing suspiciously alone in its view that Jesus' work and message manifest a supernatural Redeemer. But New Testament scholarship now repudiates the old modernist notion that the Synoptic Gospels present us only with a human Jesus whose work and teaching define the Kingdom of God but not with Christ's divine nature. The promotion of a divine Kingdom alongside the rejection of Jesus as divine King has become the theological tragedy of both the Jewish and of the Christian world. On the one hand multitudes of modern Israelis now look upon the new nation of Israel as the emerging messianic kingdom, while repudiating or ignoring Jesus of Nazareth as their promised Messiah. On the other hand, many Christians who formally acknowledge Jesus as the Divine Son of God nonetheless project only a socio-political kingdom like that sought by the ancient Pharisees alongside their rejection of the suffering Redeemer. Wherever the Kingdom is bifurcated into this distinction between God and His Christ, usurpers can too easily mount the unoccupied throne and set themselves up as lord. "I am come in my Father's name and ye receive me not," said Jesus; "if another shall come in his own name, him shall ye receive" (John 5:43). The choice facing modern man is not whether or not he will yield his life to a controlling power; it is rather, to *whose* power he in fact does actually yield dominion over his life. Men who will not have Jesus as King invariably have some other king than Jesus.

The Kingdom is indeed God's Kingdom. *"Thine* is the Kingdom" means emphatically that man is neither its projector nor preserver nor protector. It is God's Kingdom, promised by the prophets and brought near to fallen man and unveiled by and in Jesus Christ. In the life of Jesus the Kingdom is most conspicuously present in history. He proclaimed the Kingdom of God "at hand," because the King Himself was now personally present in the midst of men. In His very person the Kingdom of God had already come. His own life and work perfectly mirrored the rule of God in the stream of human history. "This is my beloved Son, in whom I am well pleased."

And wherever Jesus is acknowledged in human life as Lord and Saviour, there the Kingdom of God is most conspicuously present in world history. The closest approximation of the Kingdom of God today is the Church, the body of regenerate believers that owns the crucified and risen Redeemer as its Head. It is God's Kingdom, and we who know His Son know that, as Paul writes, He "hath delivered us from the power of darkness, and hath translated us into the kingdom of his dear Son" (Colossians 1:13).

2. *What is the Kingdom?* It is God's manifested authority and power throughout His creation; it is God's rule in the lives of redeemed men and women; and finally it includes God's full subjugation of evil and His glorious reign on earth as in heaven.

The glitter of the pseudo-kingdom lies in the injustices they boldly promise to erase, and in the utopian counter-proposals they offer the unthinking masses without a real demand for man's spiritual decision.

There is *Communism*'s offer of a politico-economic kingdom. Against exploitation of the worker, against exploitation of the poor, against the undisciplined life, one can say much that the Marxists say. But the Biblical prophets said it long before the Marxists, and said it better. For Communism substitutes a worse exploitation; it reduces man to an instrument of the state; it deprives the worker and the poor alike of human rights deriving from the divine image in man; and the kingdom it offers turns out on examination to be anti-Christ in character.

There is *Scientism*'s offer of an experimental golden age. Against ancient superstitions that survive in man's religions, against the medieval magic found even in some of the churches, against suspicion of scientific inquiry and indifference to new ways of doing things, science says much with which we must agree. But where is pagan superstition deplored, where is man's real dominion over the earth encouraged, where is the intelligibility of the space-time world asserted more than in the inspired Hebrew-Christian writings? But Scientism has shaped an arsenal of power unharnessed by moral imperatives while it has cast needless doubt on the central miracles of revealed religion. Therefore the kingdom of creature comforts it offers in the new world of speed and space turns out in spirit, if not in intention, to be anti-Christ.

There is *Existentialism:* a kingdom of unprincipled subjectivity, of free decision. Against man's loss of the present in the past, against the downgrading of human decision, against the scientific viewing of man in machine-like predictabilities, existentialism says much that is valuable. Yet nowhere is the importance of human decision more clearly affirmed than in Scripture: "Behold, now is the acceptable time; behold, now is the day of salvation" (2 Corinthians 6:2). Existentialism mistakenly places man at the center of the universe, it rejects the objective reality of the supernatural God, and it ignores His rational revelation. Making every man lord of his own life, existentialism propounds a kingdom that turns out in spirit to be anti-Christ.

Though at times these spurious kingdoms fly the colors of the Kingdom of God, they are foredoomed to failure because of their misplaced confidence in fallen man and their rejection of the redemption that is in Christ Jesus. They are the latest fashions in the parade of man-made utopias inaugurated by the theology of unbelief.

Many liberal theologians at the turn of the century dissociated Christianity from "pious" concepts such as the Kingship of God and the Kingdom of Heaven. Such notions were declared out of step with the modern democratic outlook and hence dispensable; the ancient Biblical writers were said to have borrowed them from despotic pagan governments. Presumably the Christian cause could be enhanced were God not viewed as King but as President. Since a president's tenure depends upon popular election, the Kingdom of God would then acquire the plasticity of a party caucus. No longer was the Kingdom distinctive found in Jesus' regeneration of lost individuals; instead, the "moral influence of Jesus" in public affairs, and then the socio-political influence of churchmen espousing legislative programs in His name, soon became the essence of Christian relevance.

Today Christendom is saturated with the slogans of ersatz kingdoms that borrow their imagery from the Kingdom of God. Communists have become past-masters of this art, but their disavowal of the supernatural somewhat discourages using a Christian label to promote their secular goals. American politicians, however, are increasingly given to this sort of expropriation, although happily American politicians have not yet yielded to the European and Latin American readiness to label their political parties as Christian. But such slogans as "back to normalcy," "the new deal," "the new frontier," and the "great society" have little in common with the normalcy, newness and greatness that stands in the forefront of Jesus' teaching. Lest somebody think my aim is to downgrade the Democrats, I should add that Republicans are not immune to this same temptation; recently they have had less opportunity to yield to it, and when they do their hallucinations seem more modest. Washington is a land of rich reward for ghost writers who can impart credulity to ghost kingdoms, and sustain the lively hope of a materialistic millennium for a generation of plastic souls. We pass from one era of political propaganda to another while society remains abnormal, or becomes more so; while the masses remain unsatisfied with what is newly dealt them. The new frontiers revive the same old problems, and the new society perpetuates the immorality and criminality of the old.

When Jesus preached the Kingdom of God He warned His disciples against hungering for the bread that perishes. He indicated the ultimate destiny of these political kingdoms: "For nation shall rise against nation, and kingdom against kingdom" (Matthew 24:7). Already in our time the entire earth trembles on the dawn of a global Nagasaki or Hiroshima, yet we blithely ignore every warning of destruction by the God of the atom.

The Kingdom of God demands an inner change—not simply an external rearrangement or environmental readjustment. However hopefully as philosophers and politicians may speak of an ideal society, without this moral and spiritual rebirth men remain in the gloom of night. Christ demands conversion at the threshhold of His Kingdom. "Except ye be converted . . . ye shall not enter into the Kingdom" (Matthew 18:3). "Except a man be born again he cannot see the Kingdom of God" (John 3:3). That is the very first distinctive of God's Kingdom: without spiritual rebirth no man can share in it.

In discussing our theme I want to give special attention

to a volume written at the turn of the century by Sidney L. Gulick on *The Growth of the Kingdom of God* (Chicago, Student Missionary Campaign Library, and New York, Revell, n.d.) and translated into Japanese in an attempt to persuade Japanese students to become Christians. The author of *The Growth of the Kingdom of God* was more restrained than many later champions of the social gospel; Jesus, he admits, did not expect the Kingdom to completely eliminate wickedness in this world. Yet Gulick's argument is based on the perceptible growth of the Kingdom of God in the expansion of Christian influence and in the increase of church adherents. In the closing decades of the last century Jesus' influence was said to be "spreading in every land and on every shore" and through spontaneous influence this "Kingdom of God, of Love, of Truth . . . shall ever more progress 'with the progress of the sun.' " Predictably increasing *numbers* will come to believe Christ's teaching, their *understanding* of this teaching will deepen, their reflection of Christ's *spirit* will multiply, and their teaching will increasingly Christianize even those who make no personal claim to believe.

"During the (first) ninety years of the religious history of the United States," Gulick wrote, "more persons have come under the direct influence of the Christian Church than during the first thousand years of Christianity in all lands combined" (pp. 163 f.). In 1980 the Protestant population in the United States was only 22.6% and the Roman Catholic population only 11.5%, but measuring "the expansion of the Kingdom of God by the leaven of influence," he contended, Christianity could count on 56.6% of the rest of the population as Christian "adherents," and only 9.3% as pagan.

Gulick further declared that "the present generation seems to have the advantage over every preceding one, not only in its national, but also in its spiritual civilization in

understanding the great problems of life, in comprehending
the nature of religious truth, in recognizing God's actual
presence in the world, and in doing His will. . . . Most of
the Christians of the early centuries, . . . even of the first
century, knew less . . . of the actual teachings and life of
Christ than is known today by the ordinary Protestant. . . .
With the exception of the apostles themselves and a few of
the earliest disciples, I am confident that the average Protestant Christian of today has a better appreciation, both of
what Christ came to do and of the nature of the salvation
He offers, than had the mass of Christians of any previous
century" (*ibid.,* pp. 169-170).

We need not wholly debunk Gulick's emphasis. The
Protestant Reformation had restored to multitudes the
realities of apostolic Christianity which the Middle Ages
had concealed. An awakening Protestant missionary concern had ushered in a century of Christian expansion. In
the fond hope of evangelizing all men everywhere in a
single generation, evangelicals carried the Gospel to every
part of the earth. In Protestant lands the system of general
education and the universal diffusion of the Bible through
modern printing techniques acquainted multitudes with
the message of Christ. Sunday schools sprang up everywhere
to acquaint believers with the Bible, which had never before
been in the hands of so many people. The twentieth century
was indeed poised for unparalleled Christian advance.

But that great opportunity was forfeited by the unfortunate deployment of Christian leadership, institutions, and
resources to the abortive social gospel. Gulick's argument
for *The Growth of the Kingdom of God* in Japan is a mirror
on much of Anglo-Saxon as well as Asian Protestantism in
one strategic sector of the Orient. The initial impact of
evangelical missionaries upon Japan had indeed been phenomenal, but very little fruit of the Christian witness remains

in Japan in the aftermatch of three generations of domi-
nantly liberal Protestant ministry.

The reasons for this miscarriage of the Church's mission
are illuminating and instructive.

Gulick contended that there had been a progressive increase from 5 million nominal Christians at the end of
the third century to 500 million at the end of the nineteenth
who accepted Christian moral standards. "Never was Christianity growing so rapidly in numbers as now (about
1890)," wrote Gulick. Thus virtually equating Christianity
with nominal adherence, he celebrated "the number of
those who . . . may properly be called Christian, that is to
say, the number of those who are living under Christian
standards and ideals of moral life and conduct, whether
professedly followers of Christ or not" *(ibid.,* p. 23). He
boasted that 55 per cent of the world population was already
"governed by Christian races" due not simply to colonial
conquest, but especially to "the prodigious natural growth
of the Christian nations" *(ibid.,* p. 24). "The Christian
powers have increased the territory under their rule from
about 7 per cent of the surface of the world in 1600 to 82
per cent in 1893, while the non-Christian powers have
receded from about 93 per cent to about 18 per cent during
the same period. At present the Protestant nations alone
rule about twice as much territory as all the non-Christian
nations combined" *(ibid.,* p. 28). "The governments of
Christian races far exceed those of non-Christian races in
ideals (and) in impartiality. . . ." *(ibid.,* p. 24). Legislated
benevolence, moreover, was heralded as "truly Christian"
and "due to the growing power of the Kingdom of truth
and righteousness" (p. 121). Gulick found "remarkable
evidence of the growth of the Kingdom" in public education as the friend rather than foe of the religious life, and
in the improvement of "character" that had reduced the

number of convicted criminals 75 per cent (p. 118). Ex-
pecting the twentieth century to fulfill the vision of righteousness on earth, Gulick told Japanese intellectuals that
they had best swim with the tide of the future, because the
Christian inundation of the West would almost inevitably
transform the Orient. "The Kingdom of Heaven is growing,
and never so fast as in the last decades of the nineteenth
century"—particularly in it social and political ideals.

What evidence had liberals in proof of their claims that
the Kingdom of God was assuming world-wide proportions
at the beginning of our century?

Here were Gulick's sure signs of the ballooning Kingdom:
The doctrine of the brotherhood of man was now familiar
"the world over." Not professing Christians only but "all
the people of Christendom" now held human life in sacred
regard. Christian ideals had "transformed savage, bloody,
brutal, pagan Europe . . . into modern, law-abiding, comparatively peaceful nations." Not only in theory but largely
in practice the "life of every man" had now become of
equal value. In place of war international abritration was
being tried with marked success. In summary, "the Church
and the Christspirit" had become "the strongest influences
making for international peace and good-will on earth" (p.
261). Only liquor dealers and some unions opposed legislation to enforce Sunday rest. Christ's influence was growing
century after century in the world of literature. Even the re-
jecters of Christianity virtually admitted the truth and authority of Christ's teachings—so he argued—and the world
of scientific thought was pro-Christian: "The scientific mind
of the civilized world is as fully convinced of the truth of all
that is important in Christianity as it ever was, and . . . and
devoted as ever to the attainment of real Christian character." Jesus' influence had spread far beyond the limits of
Christendom; India and Japan had been "wonderfully

modified" and "elevated" by Christian ideals; in Japan,
Christian ideals had "already so permeated the institutions
and populations" that Christianity was "a creative energy
in politics, industry, and learning." "It is safe to say," wrote
Gulick, "that the Gospel of Christ, and love for the Saviour
of mankind, are spreading more rapidly among non-Christian communities during the nineteenth century than at any
previous time, not even excepting the first and second
centuries" (p. 289). Could any hearer doubt that the
Kingdom of God on earth was at long last just around
the corner?

We do not dispute the fact that alongside its redemption
of individuals the Gospel of Christ had bestowed inestimable
benefits upon civilization. Biblical religion brings the sanction of revelation to those ethical imperatives by which
Christianity has now and again lifted men to the loftiest
virtues in human history. But this by-product of revealed
religion does not justify a liberal misunderstanding of the
Kingdom of God that revises Jesus' teaching and aims only
to reconstruct the social order by registering Christian
influences upon unregenerate mankind. This distortion sees
the world as God's Kingdom, viewed as a mixture of persons truly Christian, nominally Christian, and potentially
Christian. In Biblical theology the Kingdom is in the world
but not of it, the Kingdom is in the mixture; whereas, in
liberal theology, the mixture is in the Kingdom.

Consider how this social gospel has distorted the Bible
and confused the churches. Here are four of its features
with which evangelical Christians must still contend:

1. The view that the unregenerate heathen are lost is
held to contradict Christ's own spirit and His teaching of
love. So the contrast between true Biblical religion and
false religion is displaced. All world religions are said to
contain more or less truth, more or less revelation and

inspiration. The Christian missionary movement has lost its momentum wherever this revisionist theology has permeated it.

2. The Biblical doctrines of the wrath of God and the final doom of the wicked are set aside because of modern speculation about God's limitless mercy and the matchless sympathy of Jesus.

3. The miracles are no longer emphasized; even the bodily resurrection of Christ is ignored. Rather, stress falls on the moral majesty of Christ, and the moral truth of Christianity—that is, on Christianity's internal character—to preserve "relevance for the Gospel in a scientific age." Liberals speak confidently of Christ's moral majesty even while their New Testament scholars elsewhere declare the Gospels to be untrustworthy historical records and liberal oratory can twist this moral truth into pacifism, socialism, or some other ism nowhere discoverable in Jesus' teaching. Historic Christian theology is set aside; the great creeds are supposedly honored as simple expressions of religious piety and devotion, while they are rejected as statements of religious truth. The major goal of Christendom then becomes organic church union. Denominational distinctives seem wholly insignificant when one views as dispensable the larger beliefs that Protestant denomination had held in common since the Reformation.

4. A new attitude then arises toward society, a shift of ecclesiastical strategy due to more optimistic theories of human nature. Redemptive regeneration is no longer thought necessary to alter the main course of history, and liberalism looks instead to the social sciences as a lever to establish the Kingdom of God on earth. In Jesus' teachings churchmen like Gulick located the "noblest foundation" and "greatest impulse" for the social sciences, and in their emergence found evidence that "more and more the teach-

ing of Christ is prevailing, that His Kingdom is coming.
. . . Never before were the signs of growth of Christianity
so manifest as they are today, or the growth itself so rapid"
(ibid., pp. 197ff.). While the Church may exist ideally
where redeemed sinners unite to worship Christ and to
obey His commands, the "growth" of the Kingdom no
longer depends on the divine gift of repentance and regeneration. Rather, "the influence of Christ's teachings on the
world, on those who make no profession of being Christ's
disciples" *(ibid.,* p. 241), holds the stage. Two theses are
then added—that churchgoers should organize public and
national life on specifically Christian principles, and that
persons inside or outside the Church who are attracted to
Christ's life and teachings are to be reckoned as true Christians *(ibid.,* p. 241). Jesus' influence was now so "dominant
in Christendom," we were told, that "it is no more possible
for a man who lives in a Christian nation and society to
escape this influence than it is for him to escape . . . the
force of gravitation that holds him to the earth" (pp. 245 f).

Surely it would have shocked Gulick and his hearers
had they seen a preview of the twentieth century. Regarded
as a liability was to be the prodigious natural growth of
the races he hailed as a Christian by-product and as an
asset; and nominally Christian colonial governments too
were to be regarded as a hindrance to the spread of the
Gospel. Gulick's prediction of the universal triumph of
Christian truth and love was to be overrun by World War I;
and then by the barbarian Nazis with their murder of
six million Jews; by the Japanese bombing of Pearl Harbor
and the American counter bombing of Nagasaki and Hiroshima. The formal Orthodox Christianity of Russia, and
the Lutheranism of German Saxony as well were to fall
before Communists whose government champions the welfare state while it thwarts Christianity. Britain and Sweden

welcome socialism while church attendance sags, and the new state of Israel embraces many socialist features while the Israelis remain ardently non-Christian.

I warn you in Jesus' name that all the non-scriptural kingdoms are a mirage. Jesus preached a Kingdom with eternal foundations, a Kingdom that endures forever. We need to hear Jesus reminding Pilate: "My Kingdom is not of this world." We need desperately to learn anew that the Kingdom is not Christendom as such; it is not the visible Church as such; it is not the ecumenical movement, nor any denomination inside or outside that movement, or all these denominations together. The Kingdom of God is the rule and reign of God; it is manifested in the midst of men in Jesus Christ; it is mirrored in the fellowship of the redeemed who seek to do God's will on earth; and it is soon to come in power and great glory in the crowning climax of human history.

3. *When is the Kingdom?* Jesus taught clearly that, in some tremendous sense, the Kingdom of God is *now* for everyone who receives Him as Saviour and Lord. There is more to the Biblical view of the Kingdom than that it is *now,* but the sense in which the Kingdom is *now* for all who know the Redeemer is highly important. Jesus Christ did not leave a vacuum in human history and in human experience into which tyrants are free to insert their totalitarian claims over human life on the ground that nobody else legitimately occupies the throne of the universe. Those totalitarian dictators are squatters on the King of Glory's terrain. We who own Jesus Christ as Lord and Saviour know that no other man dare wield an absolute claim over humanity, for Christ alone is King of kings and Lord of lords, He alone is the Lord of truth, He alone is Lord of life. "*Lord*—what wouldest thou have me to do?" was Paul's cry on the Damascus Road, and likewise it must

be modern man's cry in the wilderness of contemporary life if we too are to find sight in our blindness.

The Kingdom of God is a new dimension of life—not, as philosophers are prone to view it, simply a speculative ideal or a possibility of new knowledge. Truth has its indispensable place. Yet the Hebrew rabbi Nicodemus was quite ready to welcome some new doctrine: "We know that thou art a teacher come from God; tell us, then, [we can almost overhear him adding] what more do I need to know?" But the Kingdom is more than formal knowledge of the truth; it is personal commitment to the King of truth; it is a divine dominion under which men live; it is submission to God's sovereignty as a present reality. The Kingdom makes a present moral and spiritual demand, as Paul writes: "The unrighteous shall not inherit the Kingdom of God" (1 Corinthians 6:9). "The Kingdom of God is not meat and drink, but righteousness, and peace, and joy in the Holy Ghost" (Romans 14:17).

One way and only one way do you and I have a place in this Kingdom. The precondition of our participation is a change of nature, a new nature. The Pharisees wrongly thought their Jewish genealogy, their physical descent from Abraham, automatically assured their status in the Kingdom. "We are Abraham's sons" (John 8:33), they insisted; Jesus was equally insistent that their hostility to Him showed them rather to be children of the Devil. The medieval Church of Rome wrongly taught that receiving the sacraments automatically makes one a child of the Kingdom merely in terms of environmental transformation. The nominal Christian mistakes church attendance or membership with a place in God's Kingdom. But the condition for our participation in the Kingdom is regeneration by the Spirit of God. "Except a man be born again," said Jesus, "he cannot see the Kingdom of God" (John 3:3). "Except ye be converted, and become as little children, ye shall not enter into the Kingdom of heaven" (Matthew 18:3). Only regenerate sinners have a place in God's Kingdom.

The churches today are overrun with members who remain outside the door of Christ's Kingdom. They are strangers to His redemptive love and regenerative power; they are unswayed by His sovereign rule and have no sure destiny in eternity. Something is radically wrong with a local church whose members formally claim to know Christ as Lord, and yet almost never enlist others or even attempt to enlist them as believers. We sing "like a mighty army moves the Church of God," but an army that captures only one or two stragglers a year is hardly worth the name. The reason churchgoers are not evangelizing the earth, the reason they are not taking the Great Commission seriously, is that they themselves have never been evangelized. They are part of the Church's problem, part of the Church's predicament, rather than the answer to the world's dilemma. Multitudes in the church have never led another person to Christ, and multitudes seem not really to have found Christ for themselves.

Let us, then, behold in brief summary the great turning points of the glorious Kingdom of God. Jesus preached the imminent coming of that Kingdom; it was "at hand" in history; it was dawning in His own ministry, and His life and work revealed it as a present fact. What had been concealed, the incarnate King of love now disclosed. He came to offer us a place in His Kingdom, and through the obedient devotion of twice-born men to show the power and authority of the King from age to age. He rules even the unregenerate world by preserving it in being against a great day of reckoning; by His Biblically published moral principles mankind will finally be judged, and only by

obedience to His precepts can any civilization long hope to
endure. There is more. The fulness of His Kingdom will
come at last not through man's self-effort but like lightning
slashing from heaven: it will be eschatological. Now God's
Kingship is reflected on the historical scene only in a broken
way in the remnants of justice and peace, but its sure consummation will mark the judgment of all the nations. The
King Himself will return in glory to proclaim the end of all
the kingdoms of this world. Then indeed, "the kingdoms
of this world are become the Kingdom of our Lord, and of
His Christ; and He shall reign for ever and ever" (Revelation 11:15). The reign of God will come—the vindication
and triumph of righteousness and the eternal bliss of the redeemed, the subjugation and doom of evil, and the final
judgment of the wicked. Every knee shall bow to the King
of kings, to the Lord of lords. Those who wait for the
triumph of the proletariat to crown the historical order will
find that it is His judgment the proletariat faces. Those
who confuse the spread of democracy with the extension
of the Gospel will likewise be put to shame. Thine is the
Kingdom! It is Christ's Kingdom. By the new birth we are
offered a place in it now, and this divine work of saving
grace alone introduces men to life that is truly life and
qualifies men for a glorious destiny in eternity.

I was walking in Brussels, Belgium, a few years ago
with one of my former theological students, now a second
generation missionary. Suddenly he stopped in his tracks
and said: "We have just come to 'the street of one man';
we must walk through it one at a time, because it's too
narrow for more than one." By the atoning work of
Christ and the regenerating work of the Holy Spirit every
giant and pygmy of this world must pass if ever he finds
that abundant life of which Jesus spoke. Jesus likened the
Kingdom to the merchant "who sells all that he has to

possess the pearl of great price." But in our affluent society men barter everything for very poor pearls or for no pearl at all; the saddest fact about our twentieth century is that the midgets and the mighty in our time remain strangers to the Kingdom that is forever. The Kingdom of heaven remains the most neglected commodity in our free market economy. You have an opportunity, before men and angels, and before God Himself, to show by your decision and deeds that Christ and His Kingdom remain the most precious treasure in human life and experience.

Chapter VII

EDUCATION AND RELIGION
IN EVANGELICAL PERSPECTIVE

There's a story making the rounds in Washington about a modern jigsaw puzzle. It seems a distraut mother was waiting patiently for her fidgety teen-ager's seance with the local psychiatrist. In the waiting room the frustrated youngster had tried frantically for almost an hour to piece together the patchwork puzzle. Finally the mother appealed to the office secretary: "Show her how to do it," she pleaded, "before she blows her stack!" "Oh," said the secretary, "that game is supposed to get people adjusted to the twentieth century; *there's no way whatever to make the pieces fit.*"

A major characteristic of the intellectual world in the late twentieth century is the divorce and apparent irreconcilability of education and religion. The importance of this development is sensed only by those who know the history of thought, and who are familiar with the remarkable impact in earlier generations of the Christian religion upon the Western world.

The followers of Jesus Christ challenged the many ancient pagan religions in the name of God's special redemptive revelation, proclaiming the monotheism of the Bible to be the one true religion. In asserting this claim of the Gospel toward every member of the human race, Christianity in time became the mother of popular education. The ancient Greeks and Romans had no passion either to evangelize or to educate the world. But no movement committed to any other ideology in the history of thought was motivated as was evangelical Christianity by its devotion to the truth of revelation toward the evangelization and education of the human race. If the living God has published the criteria by which men and nations will ultimately be judged, if Jesus Christ is the only saving name, and if Jesus' parting message spurred His disciples to carry the good tidings of salvation to the ends of the earth, His loyal followers had no option but to teach His commandments universally.

The inherited religion of the West, therefore, stamped upon the medieval and early modern mind a firm confidence in the inherent unity of education and religion. Christianity affirms, in fact, that all enlightenment proceeds from the true and living God, and that the Holy Spirit employs truth as a means of persuasion. From Augustine through Calvin the great Christian thinkers of the West expounded the Christian faith in terms of true religion, and the early modern and some recent philosophers from Descartes and Locke to Hegel and Hocking crowned their speculative systems with an acknowledgment that God is the ultimate reality, the inherently holy, and the ground of truth.

It is no secret that most formative intellectual centers in our century have now dissolved this ultimate unity of the true and the holy. While popular education once recognized Christianity as its mother, yet the academic world has somehow come to treat supernatural religion as a disaffected mother-in-law and finally as an outlaw. We shall not long pause over the details of this breakup of a long-standing matrimony except to mention a few of its explosive moments.

If Christian truth about God and man supplied in medieval and early modern times the integrating principle of the university world, in the nineteenth century that role was optimistically captured by the autonomous human reason and the spirit of free inquiry. For more than a generation German higher critics had invoked science and evolution in the same breath to discredit the supernatural so that by World War I, as Rudolf Eucken reported, university students greeted their professors' religion with sustained applause. The attack was not confined to the scriptural attacks on supernatural religion of special creation and special redemption; it was extended also to philosophical idealism stripped of miraculous features, so that supernaturalism of the pre-Christian Greek and Roman sort was equally under attack. A world-renowned modernist like Albert Schweitzer soon lamented the fact that ethical religion and modern thought no longer constitute a unified spiritual force.

Indeed, religion *per se,* whichever variety dared claim universal validity, now came under attack. Anglo-Saxon humanists curiously contended that religion is benevolent while they malevolently dissolved God into social ideals. The zealous Russian Communists meanwhile sought to discredit religion as such; their "opiate of the masses" verdict assigned religion an intellectually significant role only insofar as it served to implement their revolutionary social objectives. In Germany, Tübingen professor Wilhelm Hauer tapered religion to nationalistic significance; contending that religious experience is relative to national temperament, he proposed a new German religion. Tolerance implies, he said, that no religion can be granted universal validity.

In America, John Dewey and other humanists founded

public educational philosophy on a naturalistic view of the world and life intolerant of supernatural being; over and above ethical concerns they allowed no status to religious realities except in man's emotions or volition. It was Robert Hutchins' impatience with this dogmatism that in the early 1940's sent naturalists at the University of Chicago fleeing from the exacting philosophy department to the less exacting divinity school. In those dark days the divinity school not only gave sanctuary to naturalists, but discouraged theological students from pursuing doctoral studies if they were convinced supernaturalists.

In the public schoolroom, too, God became a controversial subject best banned from the learning process. For one generation a progressively vague religious reality was tolerated in worship exercises, but the secularist zeal for total separation of church and state soon eliminated even this remnant of a devout tradition, and separation of education from religion was then virtually complete.

Just as pressures had mounted against the recognition of the reality of God in public education, so now they are mounting against any recognition of the reality of God in public life, and hence for separation of the state from God. In practice, segregation of the public sector from religious manifestations is not yet as complete as some secularists wish it were. The spiritual tradition survives in the chaplaincy both in Congress and in the military; in the schoolroom flag salute, with its prepositional phrase "under God"; in the market place where our coins at least carry assurance that it is God rather than American fiscal policy we trust.

But the great divorce has left permanent scars upon both the ecclesiastical and the educational arenas; and conspicuously so at their points of confluence. As recent Danforth Foundation surveys clearly indicate, church related colleges have moved in two directions. The most powerful academic institutions have tended to become explicitly secular, while the most devout spiritual institutions have tended to become intellectually introvert. In a word, the church college campuses readily took sides either as loss-of-faith campuses, or as defender-of-tradition establishments.

If most of the leaders of the Protestant Reformation were university-trained scholars, now most university scholars could not care less, either about the Protestant Reformation or about the Christian revelation. Were the question of belief in God to be decided by a reference to the world of modern culture we would today be driven into the camp of unbelief. The staggering enterprise of technological science seems to find God dispensable; the international political arena moves from crisis to crisis as if God were useless; and the economic world faces its herculean problems as if God were an extraneous consideration. In modern decisions God may not be dead, as some theological sensationalists would have it, but in public affairs He is an obvious irrelevance—and He more and more becomes so also in the modern intellectual's formulation of a program of life.

An assistant professor of humanities in Stanford University, Michael Novak, reminds us bluntly that "the man in tune with our culture does not believe in God" *(Belief and Unbelief,* New York, The Macmillan Company, 1965, p. 41). "It is impossible for one who believes in God to work in the intellectual world of the United States without becoming aware that among intellectuals the bias of the age" tilts against such belief. "A great many of one's philosophical associates, and certainly the most articulate, are agnostics or atheists". . . . "Large numbers of philosophers, psychologists, and social scientists seem to be quite certain that such faith is unintelligent and mythical" *(ibid.,* pp. 16, 193). Again, "It is taken for granted in most intellectual circles that an intelligent person does not believe in God. . . . Given the general panorama of belief in God in America and the life of institutional religion in America, the young person is inevitably attracted to unbelief" *(ibid.,* pp. 35 f.). "For the first time in human history," Novak adds, the best minds in the West have "made unbelief a chosen project of the human will, and on a large scale" *(ibid.,* p. 36). "The thesis of intellectual life in America is that there is no God. A man seems foolish to dissent" *(ibid.,* p. 57).

If this were the verdict of a fundamentalist minister pronouncing external judgment upon the academic community, indignant denials could likely be expected from professional educators. But it is a Stanford professor to whom educators must reply if any case can still be made for the contrary thesis that intellectual pressures in the world of liberal learning favor faith in the supernatural. While the climate of the classroom remains so widely swept by the winds of modernity, it is highly unlikely that anybody will wish to contract out for this job of preparing a rebuttal.

Although temporal and material concerns preoccupy many of their professors, a noteworthy development is discoverable within the new generation of students. The professors belong largely to a generation that forsook the God of their fathers and saw Biblical religion as a lost cause. But most students now belong to a generation whose fathers had no fixed spiritual moorings and no sure cause, and many students are increasingly determined not to inherit the vacuums and disillusionments of the older generation. By such students the question of faith is being resurrected with new zeal.

Novak likewise tells us that as a generation ago there

was "a crisis of belief," so now "a crisis of unbelief" has dawned. "The unbeliever speaks of his temptation to succumb to 'a failure of nerve.' Young people, brought up by nonbelieving parents, are raising again the question of God, just as their parents, brought up by believing parents, cleansed their minds of it" (*ibid.*, p. 20). He describes "many hundreds of thousands of young Americans (who) are not satisfied with their parent's views of life. . . . They are torn by interior movements both of belief and unbelief, believing in a kind of God on Mondays, Wednesdays, and Fridays, and warning themselves against illusions, a failure of nerve, and intellectual cowardice on the other days. They do not know which way to turn; their enlightenment has proved empty and fallacious, but the religious thought they encounter is unintelligent. Like the dry leaves of the *Inferno,* they blow back and forth in the empty spaces outside the gates of heaven and hell" (*ibid.,* p. 36).

These signs of rising religious interest have so disturbed some naturalists at the professorial level that one scholar, Dr. Paul Edwards of New York University, has collected Bertrand Russell's essays against religion in order to restate the case for unbelief. In his introduction to the paperback volume *Why I Am Not a Christian* by Bertrand Russell (New York, Simon and Schuster, 1957), Edwards curiously contends that in the university world the question of belief or unbelief is currently biased toward belief, and he complains that only the "better colleges," as he labels them, now present the case against belief *(ibid.,* p. xii).

What can confidently be said is hardly that the world of liberal learning today propagandizes for faith in the supernatural, since most academic pressures obviously remain directly or indirectly naturalistic. But we do seem to observe a new courtship between education and religion. On many campuses, even at state universities, there is a fresh probing of the possibility and responsibility of teaching religion in the classroom. A school of religion has emerged on such state campuses as Indiana, Iowa, Kansas, Missouri, Montana, and Wyoming, while Illinois, Minnesota, and Wisconsin are studying the feasibility of a department of religious studies. The public elementary and high schools too, however hesitantly, are again looking at proposals for teaching religion on some basis, if only in order to understand the cultural heritage of the Western world.

But this trial marriage of education and religion now embraces new and noteworthy factors. If the American colonial colleges arose within the conviction that Christianity as the one true religion provides the *integrating* factor in the realm of learning, in the present academic scene religion mainly serves as an *additive* to the liberal arts curriculum. Many sociology textbooks still accord religion no decisive place in man's experience, but rather assign it only peripheral significance. The introduction of religion courses serves no correlating function in the areas of liberal learning, but tends rather to increase the diversity of views and to leave faith hanging in mid-air. While education is championed as the serious pursuit of truth, nowhere more than in the religious realm does the liberal arts campus today seem skeptical over any attainment of truth.

Much of this spiritual agnosticism had earlier roots in Protestant modernism's rejection of the possibility of man's cognitive knowledge of transcendent Being, a disavowal that deprives faith in the supernatural world of any claim to truth. With this development the intellectual synthesis of education and religion was broken. The contemporary campus has made no assured recovery from this breach. Even the church colleges today tend to duplicate the failure of the non-religious campuses to comprehensively integrate the content of learning in terms of a rationally unified view of life and the world. It would be hard to overestimate the cost of this delinquency. College students may hitchhike a thousand miles and demonstrate day and night for the cause of social integration, but if they venture into the modern conflict for men's minds without coherently integrating the claims of pure religion and of academic learning, they will simply perpetuate in themselves the logical and psychological instability that haunts the larger intellectual world in our time.

One noteworthy development of modern religious thought is that religious modernism, after first forfeiting the faith in rational revelation for a philosophy of rationalism, has now widely espoused religious irrationalism. The harm done at the frontiers of religious education by this irrationalistic tendency can hardly be overestimated. Emphasize the unity of *experience* though it may, the unity of *truth* is precisely what Protestant modernism has progressively surrendered for a century. For all his perverse rationalism, the philosopher Hegel retained as a sound inheritance from Biblical religion an emphasis on the essential unity of the truth of philosophy and the truth of religion. But this emphasis was banished into outer space by the modernism of Kant and Ritschl, the dialectical theology of Barth and Brunner, and the existential theology of Bultmann.

A few months before Albert Schweitzer's death I had a personal note from that influential modernist of the recent past. To the last Schweitzer retained a great conviction about reason and religion that many of his contemporaries had come to abandon—the historic Judeo-Christian conviction that the truth of education and the truth of religion—all truth, in fact—is one truth. An evangelical may rightly complain that Schweitzer no doubt failed to do full justice to the reality of revelation and instead allowed pantheistic philosophy to color his assessment of life and culture. But

contemporary education and religion alike need to redis-
cover his awareness that the truth of religion and the truth
of philosophy must be one and the same truth. When
Schweitzer died, *Christianity Today* quoted his comment
on the sad stance of Christianity in the world of modern
thought: "The religion of our age," he wrote, "gives the
same impression as an African river bed in the dry season—
a great river bed, sand banks, and between, a small stream
which seeks its way. One tries to imagine that a river once
filled that bed; that there were no sand banks but that the
river flowed majestically on its way; and that it will someday be like that again."

If in our time that great river is again to flow majestically, the opportunity to abet its high tide has never con-
fronted the evangelical faith-affirming colleges as remarkably
as now.

That God is truth; that all truth is of God; that truth
is for man's obedient understanding of his Creator, for the
enrichment of man's own life, and for the greater good and
service of mankind—these emphases are integral to the
Christian view. The Christian Church historically has
regarded education and religion as complementary exposures
on the vistas of revelation; it champions therefore both
the desirability of the scholarly mind and the indispensa-
bility of the new birth. The church with an intellectually
uncircumscribed vision of reality once had a stake in the
whole truth so extensively that she became the mother
of popular education; while in her best days of moral
earnestness the campus had such a stake in spiritual realities
that learning was crowned with the knowledge of revealed
religion.

If once again the great theological and moral convictions
of Judeo-Christian religion are to become influential and
formative, the church-related colleges must fulfill a role

beyond any they now carry. In the contemporary struggle for truth, they are called to vindicate Christian convictions in a highly competitive ideological market. Precisely this opportunity to engage in the modern clash of ideas and ideals now constitutes the most exciting and demanding aspect of Christian education. As Christianity's great apostle, university-trained in Tarsus, went on to Athens to engage Stoics and Epicureans over life's ultimate issues, so evangelical educators in modern times must engage in the ideological struggle with conviction, courage, and competence.

Liberal learning surveys all the influential options on the contemporary horizon. In the modern world the alternatives to historic Christianity carry twentieth century names and nuances, and we need to relate our faith relevantly to these modern frontiers. We need to know these alternatives to faith as well as their own advocates know them—to know them through and through, as it were. We need to be skillful not only at external criticism from the standpoint of Scripture, but at internal criticism from the standpoint of intrinsic inconsistencies, of inherent weaknesses. No student achieves this ability without earnest academic engagement. A mark of a scholar is his ability to present an alien point of view fairly on its own presuppositions. We must present non-Christian theories so accurately that their advocates will marvel that this bold echo of their own convictions seems so unpersuasive to us, and we likewise will insist on such fairness in their exposition of the Christian view of God and the world that we shall not suspect that others reject what they do not really understand but only caricature. If we want the academic world to know whom we have believed, we are likely to impress others only if they are assured also that we genuinely know what we do not believe.

The religious and philosophical diversities permeating

American education are basic causes of the conflict and uncertainty on the campuses today. But there is little prospect of any return of public education to the integrating perspective and clear purpose that once shaped the American schools when Christian truth supplied unity to the curriculum and defined the goal of learning. Consciously and deliberately American colleges today embrace the pluralism of contemporary society, and even promote that pluralism under the banner of democracy and freedom. At the same time many campuses tend to exclude, sometimes consciously, sometimes unconsciously, any virile reflection of the great heritage that shaped the world of learning when American schools offered an education that was both unified and purposeful.

This pluralistic predicament of the secular colleges has now also overtaken many of the church-related campuses. But it offers the evangelical faith-affirming colleges the greatest educational opportunity in their history. The climate of religious pluralism in America is doubtless here to stay, and evangelical Christians have least to fear in a society in which spiritual decision is a matter of voluntary commitment rather than of totalitarian compulsion, whether governmental or ecclesiastical, or both. Evangelicals have always deplored the supposed furtherance of Christianity, or of any religion, by an offer of "either the sword or the Book." But in the current ideological crisis and competition, we need not, and dare not, hesitate to elaborate Judeo-Christian distinctives. We need make no apology for offering modern man the Sword of Truth and the Book, for the Judeo-Christian revelation is still worthy of our full commitment. While there are many religious traditions, there is no plurality of religious truth; either there is one body of truth, or there is none.

Let us then delineate our heritage with fidelity and

clarity. Men who profess to speak for the revealed religion
of Moses and Matthew too often sound as if they were
modern echoes of Plato, Aristotle, Kant, or Hegel. Let those
other voices be heard for what they have to say, but let
us not muffle the mind of Abraham and Moses and Isaiah
and Paul in expounding the Judeo-Christian view. The
authentic exposition of Christian truth, and of its bearing
upon modern concerns, was never more requisite than now.
Until the Christian option is considered a threat to modern
views, until those who disown it will nonetheless feel
compelled to wrestle with it in depth, until men standing
on other terrain suspect that they may ignore it to the
neglect of the claims of truth, until the "outsiders" come
and say "let us in" as spectators even if they are not yet
ready to come as champions—until then, we have not
effectively fulfilled our academic mission. The Apostle Paul
wrote that we are made "a spectacle to the world" (I Corinthians 4:9). The one thing we dare not tolerate is to be
wholly ignored. For nothing could as surely attest the
enormity of our failure in our academic mission in the
world.

If we affirm, as we assuredly do, that the Bible serves
an integrating role in liberal arts education, and is not
merely an additive, let us reflect this integration throughout
the curriculum.

Christian education is nothing if not theistic. Since the
knowledge of God crowns all other knowledge, and inter-
prets and coordinates it, Christian education must maintain
academic visibility for theology. Either "the fear of the
Lord" remains "the beginning of wisdom," or the Biblical
view reduces to antiquated superstition. While modern
man in prideful rationalism may view truth as a discovery
of reason, Christianity views truth as a revelation of God,
and reason as His created instrument. The sovereign God

of revealed religion is continually related to His world. We believe that the sense of history is not determined merely by economic forces, or by geographic or sociologic factors; we believe that man's fundamental adjustment is not to nature, as the materialists think, nor to society, as the modern sociologists and politicians seem to think, but to God.

Christian education is not simply theistic. It is trinitarian, and trinitarian theism affirms above all that the supreme revelation of God has taken place in time, in history, in His incarnate Son. If we have not brought the claims of Christian truth to visibility in this world we have failed Him doubly who stepped into time and into history, and who forces each generation of mankind to its own decision on the ultimate issues of truth and life.

This theme of the visibility of truth leads to my final comment. In traveling from campus to campus I have often asked educators about their institutional objectives. Seldom has an administrator indicated that his college seeks to give to the world persons of special character. Instead I have heard of massive building programs, of plans for a gifted faculty, of a spectacular athletic program, of the campus code, or the slant of the classroom and a special stake in the inherited tradition. For much of this I have great respect. But it was for persons that Jesus Christ came and died, and it is for persons—for the training of the most precious commodity this generation can bestow upon the future of civilization—that these institutions were founded. And it is these students and graduates who must bring the fruit of our academic labors to visibility in our time. In the arena of modern life the alumni of our evangelical institutions have never carried a more awesome responsibility than now. If to these young lives we haven't gotten across what education and religion

imply in evangelical perspective, or if they are not registering an influence in the modern world as persons, we need
to think long and hard on what it implies for religion and
education that Jesus of Nazareth is the truth incarnate.

If a former chairman of the United Nations General
Assembly, Dr. Charles Malik, has rightly assessed our times
—and I think he has, indeed, in his appraisal that "there is
an alliance, a mobilization of all the forces in the world
which hate freedom, man, God, objective truth, and the
name of Jesus Christ" then evangelical education stands
on the brink of a pagan era in which men of faith can
once more register a singular witness for God, and for
objective truth and the name of Jesus Christ, and for man
and freedom under God. God does not draft reluctant
warriors for this larger conflict; they enlist as volunteers if
they really count. And this is the hour for such volunteers.
Tomorrow may be too late.

Chapter VIII

THE ECUMENICAL AGE:
PROBLEMS AND PROMISE

Many church historians regard the ecumenical movement as the most significant development in twentieth century Christendom. It may in fact prove to be so. Yet our title refers to ecumenical promise in the singular while it speaks of ecumenical problems in the plural—a distinction that unquestionably reflects the present situation.

I.

Let me speak first, however, not of ecumenical promise or problems, but of the premise proposed by many churchmen that the ecumenical age has now already dawned. To catalogue the time-process into definitive ages is no academic novelty. In geology, for example, we speak of the age of fishes, the age of reptiles, and so on; in archaeology, pre-history advances from the stone age into the bronze age, the iron age, and then beyond. We use the same device, of course, to indicate more limited periods, as when we speak of "the age of reason," or "the age of Louis XIV" or of "the spirit of this age." I take it, then, that those who now refer to *the ecumenical age* designate not merely a temporary manifestation—something here today and gone tomorrow, as it were. They mean, rather, a decisive period in human history, an era in which Christendom itself attains full maturity—a time span in which, so to speak, the Church itself comes "of age." If that were not the case, there would be little point in inviting us to think about "the ecumenical age."

It was Dr. W. A. Visser't Hooft, an architect of the World Council of Churches, and until recently its general secretary, who perhaps first fashioned the phrase, our "semi-ecumenical age." He had in view, of course, the noteworthy reversal within twentieth century Christendom of a thousand-year process of internal division. Whereas the Eastern Orthodox Church broke from the Western Latin Church in the ninth century, the World Council of Churches now embraces Eastern Orthodoxy and large sectors of Western Protestantism. Whereas the Reformation signaled Protestant separation from the Church of Rome, Protestant-Orthodox ecumenism now includes Roman Catholicism in its intentions. With the coming of the 1960's, some ecclesiastical leaders have spoken of "the ecumenical age" and no longer simply of a "semi-ecumenical" age. For in 1961 the World Council assembly convened in non-Christian India, and brought into its membership Orthodox churchmen and churches from Communist lands. The 1963 Faith and Order Conference met in the Roman Catholic stronghold of Montreal with Orthodox participants and Catholic observers. Pope John XXIII meanwhile had convened the Second Vatican Council, launching the Church of Rome into ecumenical conversations. From this standpoint the ecumenical movement has truly come "of age." After a half-century of consolidation it breathes its own life, boasts a central committee of 100, a hierachy with an enlarging bureaucracy, and a world headquarters in Geneva.

Not all the makers of the world of tomorrow are satisfied, therefore, that our age shall become known as the "atomic age," or the "space age," or, as the Marxists would have it, "the Communist age." Those who speak instead of the ecumenical age, moreover, do not intend merely the emergence of an era of world communication and culture and a confluence of the great religions of the world. While ecumenical Christianity may indeed represent a compromise of diverse Christian traditions and a dilution of Biblical Christianity, they, nonetheless, think in terms of the universal influence of the Christian message through the visible manifestation of ecclesiastical unity.

But has ecumenism really become sufficiently influential and formative to characterize our generation in terms of *the ecumenical age?*

We are not, of course, talking about "the Church age" in the New Testament understanding of that term. The Christian religion designates as the Church age that time span from Pentecost to the second advent of Christ. The Church age has already covered more than nineteen centuries. It is not to be confused, therefore, with "the ecumenical age," which at best could only coincide with a segment of the Church age or "age of grace," in which sinners are invited to receive Jesus Christ as Saviour and Lord, thus to experience forgiveness of sins and new life. It has not remained for the twentieth century to discover that Christian "believers" constitute a supranational and supraracial fellowship—in New Testament terms, a body whose head is the crucified and risen Redeemer. The early Christians were of one "faith and doctrine," and they acknowledged one commission: to proclaim salvation in Christ to the ends of the earth. Those who thus trusted Christ staggered the ancient pagan world by their spiritual certainty, moral power, spontaneous joy, and the warmth of a fellowship that transcended distinctions of Jew and Gentile, slave and free man.

What, then, distinguishes the current ecumenical exposition of the oneness of Christ's Church from the pre-ecumenical exposition of this oneness? The term "ecumenical" means "worldwide" (from the Greek term *oikoumenē*, or "world"). The modern view locates the essence of Christian unity in a visible organic structure reflecting one world church under a single hierarchy. What was unknown in primitive Christianity during the infancy of the Church is therefore projected as a sign of ecclesiastical maturity in the ecumenical age. Hence churchmen speak today not of the Church age (in the lengthened understanding of that term), but of the ecumenical age.

This tendency is all the more remarkable because the New Testament anticipates an "end of the age" development within Christendom in terms of ecclesiastical decline rather than of maturity. Instead of charting the bright noon of the Church in history, the Bible warns of the sad eventide of the Church; rather than describing a radiant ecumenical age, it speaks of a coming "age of apostasy." With an eye on "the latter days" the Apostle Paul ranges the "mystery of godliness" unveiled in Jesus Christ alongside a "mystery of iniquity" which would all but deluge the Church of Jesus Christ. He warns against the dread effect of sin in human history. The "mystery of iniquity" reaches its zenith not outside but within the Church, which therefore reverberates with the echoes of unregenerate modes of thought and patterns of life, and in part assumes the spirit of counter-Church under the form of Church. Whereas the first disciples asked, "How can we reach the whole world with the Gospel?" the last disciples in the age of apostasy shall ask, "Will anybody be saved—even among the preachers?" As the New Testament foresees it, religious confusion shall run so rife that, were it not for God's foreclosure of human history, "the very elect" will be deceived.

We live then in the Church age. Rightly or wrongly, many Christian leaders view its contemporary materialization not in terms of an age of apostasy, but rather of the age of ecumenism. We shall consider first the problems, and then the promise, of this remarkable development.

II.

Among ecumenical problems, most observers note the external obstacles, such as the conflicting traditions, doctrinal deviations and long-standing rivalries of the major communions, and the difficulty of drawing some denominations out of isolation into dialogue. One can hardly underestimate the barrier to a universal union of churches inherent in the wide range of ecclesiastical divisions and differences, many of these now deliberately elevated to the plane of essential distinctives. Yet the fact that the ecumenical movement already embraces between 200 and 300 million Protestant and Orthodox Christians (accurate statistics are exasperatingly difficult to get) is taken as strong evidence that, problems though there be, in time ecumenism will fully win its way.

In their ecumenical analysis of problems, many champions of interchurch union concentrate on the external obstacles, and concede few if any significant weaknesses within the ecumenical movement itself. In November, 1962, *Christian Herald* published an evaluation by representative churchmen of strengths and weaknesses of the National Council of Churches. Episcopal Bishop James A. Pike, co-author with Dr. Eugene Carson Blake of the so-called Blake-Pike merger plan, could think of "no particular weakness which could not be allocated to 'growing pains'." Another ecumenist, the minister of Myers Park Baptist Church in Charlotte, North Carolina, Dr. Carlyle Marney, cited as the only "weakness" the National Council's supposed inability "to defend itself against misrepresentation" —a highly curious comment, since the journals of affiliated denominations constantly engage in ecumenical promotion.

But the problems of ecumenism are now increasingly identified not simply in terms of external indifference to the need of Christian unity, but also in terms of inner difficulties and weaknesses of the ecumenical movement and its proposals. Does the structure itself of the ecumenical movement fulfill the New Testament requirements promotive of the unity of Christian believers? Many who stand aloof from the World Council of Churches thunder a resounding no, while others remain cautiously apart. Because an effective public relations staff secures preferential treatment for ecumenism from television, radio and newspaper media, it is not usually known that the energetic National Council of Churches still does not include in its ranks some 25.6 million Protestants in the United States, or that the World Council of Churches does not include 65.3 per cent of the American missionary task force abroad.

The 10,400,000 members of the Southern Baptist Convention comprise one of the largest Protestant denominations, and it officially shuns identification with the National Council of Churches and World Council of Churches. A pointed external critique of the ecumenical movement appeared recently in *The Saturday Evening Post* ("The Ecumenical Movement Threatens Protestantism," October 24, 1964, issue) by two ordained Southern Baptist clergymen. As the Rev. Henry A. Buchanan and the Rev. B. W. Brown see it, the ecumenical movement poses a greater threat to Christendom than does the plurality of church denominations.

Their argument is cast in this form: Ecumenism "could lead to creation of an ecclesiastical power structure that bears no resemblance to anything envisioned by Jesus of

Nazareth." Protestants "may be pressured or lured into creeds and positions that will compromise their religious beliefs." Aspirations toward a superchurch "may destroy the heritage of diversity that has enriched our spiritual life." They attribute the merger momentum more to top-side ecclesiastical pressures than to spontaneous lay enthusiasm. The discounting of other doctrines to advance the doctrine of church union, they contend, may produce a "frightening form of religious bigotry" repressive of devotion to Christian truth. Ecumenical dialogue succeeds more in promoting a least common denominator theology than in securing agreement on truth; an ecumenical monopoly could thwart religious freedom. If conversations with Rome achieve union, it will be on terms favorable to the Roman pontiff; despite all his talk of "separated brethren," they warn, the Pope has recognized Protestant churches only as "communities" and not as churches.

Buchanan and Brown note that the Divine Creator set a high value on conformity and diversity alike, and they contend that the Divine Redeemer likewise displays God's glory through both the visible unity and diversity of the churches. "We are afraid," they write, "of a superchurch just as we are afraid of a superstate, and not because of a lack of faith in God. . . . Man cannot be trusted without checks and balances upon his power and authority—not even in the church. The various branches of Christendom now act as checks and balances, one upon the other, and they have a purifying effect on each other. . . . History teaches that 'the one church' soon becomes the repository of pride and power and gives very little attention to the real needs of man."

Lest such anxieties over the ecumenical movement be dismissed as a parochial viewpoint peculiar to Southern Baptists, it is noteworthy that Southern Baptists account for only 10,400,000 of the 25,600,000 Protestants remaining outside the National Council of Churches. Almost all the unaffiliated denominations recoil from the prospect of a monolithic ecclesiastical power structure whose hierarchy might negotiate commitments that outrun or violate those of their own constitutency, and find reason for these misgivings in the fact that the NCC has already neglected cherished doctrinal commitments and advocated partisan and debatable politico-economic positions.

If would be unfair, however, not to recognize that even some ardent promoters of the ecumenical movement today concede that the cause of ecumenism is sicker than most professional well-wishers care to admit. In his recent volume *Church Unity and Church Mission* (Eerdmans, 1964), Professor Martin E. Marty of the University of Chicago divinity faculty acknowledges that the movement "hasn't caught on" and "is living on borrowed time and may soon pass from favour" (p. 48). He describes it as "prematurely aged" (p. 103), and adds that it has perhaps "worked itself into a corner" (p. 59). Most of its proponents have taken a raincheck on "union now" (p. 61), he adds, and the present complications are serious enough to tempt one to despair (p. 104). Although he is associate editor of the ecumenical weekly, *The Christian Century,* Dr. Marty consoles himself with the notion that a complete reunion of Christendom is really an "eschatological hope" (p. 67)— in other words, with the awareness that the ecumenical ideal is unrealizable in present history and waits for fulfillment in the end-time.

In face of this candid internal appraisal, the notion of an ecumenical age becomes mainly a public relations illusion. Major divisions in Christendom remain to be overcome, while the extent to which ecumenical merger has actually achieved Christian unity remains to be demonstrated. The real problem does not lie only in the formidable fact that many of the world's Christians thrive outside the World Council of Churches. For despite the impressive mergers sponsored by the ecumenical movement, almost as many denominations survive inside its ranks as remain outside the movement, and their competitive tendencies appear in each annual budget.

In fact, ecumenical mergers have substituted bigger denominations for smaller denominations so that of the seven largest denominations in America, six exist within the National Council of Churches. Moreover, the emergence of these larger denominations has in turn led to a new interest in world confessionalism on a denominational basis, rather than in ecumenical nondenominationalism. Dr. Eugene Carson Blake, author of the Blake-Pike plan for American church merger, recently criticized this confessional tendency in Lutheran, Methodist, Baptist, Anglican, Presbyterian and Reformed circles.

One can, of course, scarcely blame some Protestant denominations for unwillingness to lose their identity in the World Council while Orthodox churchmen insist upon preserving theirs, or while they are unsure whether ecumenical conversations will finally blur all images except that of Rome. Yet one may ask how a denomination's formal inclusion but factual survival within the NCC or WCC actually overcomes the ecumenical contention that all denominations as such advertise Christian differences more than they safeguard Christian truth.

This denominational-ecumenical tension raises deeper issues than the desire for distinctive survival within the ecumenical context. Ministers ordained and salaried by denominations whose churches exist and thrive on the basis of denominational distinctives face increasing ecumenical pressure to work for the transformation of the very denominations in which they have taken ordination vows. Thus the denominational clergy are required to engage in a sort of double-entry ecclesiasticism. On the one hand, they promote the local church by stressing its essential distinctives alongside all other neighborhood churches; on the other hand, they are pressed to advance "central ecumenical concerns" instead of being preoccupied with the "trivia" of their own denominational life and the "housekeeping details" of their own parish. So the ecumenical movement necessarily shelters ministers who retain their denominational loyalties but either do not take the ecumenical claim seriously or do not take their denominational vows seriously. As the ecumenical movement asserts its priority over the denominational claim, ecumenism breeds a generation of young ministers who are no longer at home in their communions, who are unsure what validity if any remains in their denominational disciplines, who refer to numbers of their ministerial colleagues as "denominational hacks," and who look longingly for the death of their denominations.

Dr. Marty proposes that ecumenical churchmen contribute to the birth of "the One Great Church of the Future" by a strategy that reduces itself to ecclesiastical Machiavellianism (ibid., pp. 124 f.). He speaks of ecumenical clergymen "living in denominations and being faithful to their disciplines" while engaging in "subversion," "infiltration," "encirclement," and in other tactics which work toward "the ultimate death and transfiguration" of these forms (p. 126).

Since the clergyman does not tell his congregation or converts that he secretly strives to alter and transform the very Church with which he urges them to identify, this program of ministerial activity recommended by Dr. Marty would seem to imply the death of ecclesiastical integrity as well. If ecumenism can prosper only by this approach, even simple pragmatic considerations ought to raise the question of the essential compatibility of Christian ends and Machiavellian methods.

During the modernist-fundamentalist controversy, theoligically inclusive churchmen routinely branded as denominationally disloyal, disruptive and divisive those conservatives who protested the liberal tendency to weaken the confessional commitments of their denominations. Now the inclusivists advocate the subtle modification of church standards and the erosion of their denominations as a spiritual calling. Some who deplored as disruptive the fundamentalists who openly insisted upon doctrinal fidelity now apparently regard as virtuous the transformation of denominational theology by underground techniques.

What the Marty proposal for advancing church merger by subterranean processes reveals is the evident lack of enthusiasm for the ecumenical movement at the level of the laity. This is perhaps the greatest of all difficulties faced by the World Council of Churches. A prominent churchman in Europe remarked recently that while most church leaders there are increasingly occupied with ecumenical concerns, 95 per cent of the people couldn't care less. Local congregations protest increasingly that ministers deploy their energies to marginal concerns and neglect the ministry to which they were called.

In summary, ecumenism must contend with serious internal and external problems. Inside its own circle the ecumenical movement lacks the spontaneous enthusiasm of the laity, who increasingly resent ministerial neglect of evangelism and deplore the depreciation in the ecumenical context of denominational distinctives emphasized in the local congregation. Inclusion in the ecumenical movement has not as yet dissolved affiliated denominations, despite the insistence of some ecumenical spokesmen that demoninations are schismatic and sinful. But many clergymen are torn between pressures to foster ecumenical priorities alongside distinctive denominational responsibilities. And outside the ecumenical movement large Christian bodies interested in evangelical truth see little evidence that conservative Protestants already affiliated are influential in proportion to their numbers, and these bodies remain distrustful of the emergence of a powerful monolithic structure whose ecclesiological and theological character is unsure.

III.

If we speak of ecumenical promise, we must reckon above all with the God of promise, whose promise and fulfillment distinguish Biblical religion from non-Biblical religion. And hence we cannot escape reckoning with Jesus Christ, who is the Christian promise par excellence.

We speak readily of Christians belonging to this or that denomination, to this or that movement. But the divine promises are pledged to those who belong to God. Hear our Lord's priestly prayer: "I am . . . praying . . . for those whom thou hast given me, because they belong to thee," says Jesus. "All that is mine is thine, and what is thine is mine; and I am glorified in them" (John 17:10 f.). Their union with Christ is the presupposition of all that is expected of His followers, and their unity must reflect the unity of the Father and the Son, or it is mere human contriving. ("That they may all be one: as thou, Father, art in me, and I in thee, that they also may be in us, that the world may believe that thou hast sent me" v. 21.) This is no mere organizational affiliation, no unity only of plan and method, nor of purpose alone, but essentially a vital mystical union. To the world the true Church is visibly to manifest the love and glory of God, and this requires the disciples' spiritual and moral union with the Father and the Son.

The New Testament stresses further that the salvation of God's children scattered throughout the world requires faithful, obedient disciples. As Christ, the mediator of redemption, was God's evangelist sent from the eternal order into the historical arena, so Jesus' disciples are commissioned in His name to bear the redemptive tidings to the ends of the earth. Their manifest unity with each other is therefore both spiritually and operationally important— not simply their horizontal unity with each other, but their vertical unity with the Risen Christ: "That they may be one, as we are one; I in them, and thou in me, may they be perfectly one. Then the world will learn that thou didst send me, that thou didst love them as thou didst me" (John 17:22 f., N.E.B.). They are dispatched into the world, moreover, both as messengers of truth and mirrors of love. "Consecrate them by the truth; thy word is truth. . . . for their sake I now consecrate myself, that they too may be consecrated by the truth" (John 17:18-19, N.E.B.). The very truth of Scripture pledges their own perseverance: not one of them is lost except the son of perdition, "for scripture has to be fulfilled" (17:12, N.E.B.). So the priestly prayer locates the foundations of truth and unity in one and the selfsame Lord.

Yet modern ecumenists emphasize organizational merger above personal union with Christ and above theological unity in doctrine. The notion is widespread among them that doctrine divides while mission unites—a formula which, if fully applied, can only require efficiency in the subordination of truth. Professor Marty insists, for example, that ecumenism would soar from strength to strength if the churches would only abandon what he calls their "fruitless" policy of "truth first" (op. cit., cf. pp. 19, 61, 137 f.) and unite in a mission of "saving words and serving works" to the world.

But whoever holds reason and truth in high regard should recognize the fruitlessness of any refusal to put truth first. A refusal to put truth first may succeed in camouflaging disunity, but it cannot succeed in achieving unity. Any approach that avoids first making peace with the truth must either fall at last under the weight of error, or survive by compromising the role of reason in the realm of religion. Where commitment to truth is moderated religious affirmation becomes intellectually unimportant. If the reconciliation of ideological differences best occurs *after* union, then truth is unessential to unity. The cliché "unity first" actually plays off ecumenism against the truth. More than this, any confessionalism based on "truth later" erases Christ's promise of the Holy Spirit leading His disciples into all truth (John 16:13). While the ecumenists eloquently plead "Is Christ divided?," they themselves sunder Christ the Truth from Christ the Lord. By such abstract, conglomerate unity of Christendom the world in a remarkable way may indeed be constrained "to believe." But what it will thus be impelled to believe is something else again. Surely man may everywhere believe that, despite their violent disagreements about truth, these affiliates nonetheless all belong to the same visible organization. But the real scandal of Christianity, the blood of the Cross, is then erased along with the erasure of disunity.

In the dialogue over Christ and His Church in the world, ecumenism gives one-sided prominence to the prayer of John 17, and particularly to certain phrases. Even churchmen holding radical theories of the Bible, and still viewing the Fourth Gospel as second century embroidery of Jesus' teachings, nonetheless assume the authenticity of the prayer "that they may be one," and solemnly plead for its fulfillment in the ecumenical movement. Surely no evangelical Christian will begrudge this high regard for John 17. But, understandably, he will covet similar respect for the whole Gospel and the New Testament in its entirety.

For the Book of Revelation also comes from John's pen, and in fact contains the most extensive New Testament passage on what the Spirit said to the apostolic churches. Why is it virtually unmentioned and ignored in ecumenical circles? Here are seven churches located in Asia Minor, almost within neighborly reach of each other, and not scattered throughout distant nations. The spirit of the times was hostile, and many contrary forces marked these lonely churches for extinction. The Risen Christ held these first century churches in His right hand. What does His Spirit say, in the record of that same apostle who elsewhere gives us the Lord's priestly prayer?

Nowhere does the Spirit impose on them the priorities of twentieth century ecumenism. John greets the seven "churches" (1:4), describes his divine commission to address the seven "churches" (1:11), tells of the risen Christ who holds the seven "churches" in His hand and walks among these "churches" (1:20). Repetitiously John urges each local church to hear "what the Spirit says *to the churches*" (2:7, 11, 17, 29; 3:6, 13, 22). At least seven times, as if to punctuate the letters to the seven churches, we hear the solemn warning: "He who has an ear, let him hear what the Spirit says to the churches."

So the Lord of the Church by His Spirit speaks to the churches as authorized historical realities. And in their struggle for survival He instructs them, adding promises and warnings. Nowhere does the Risen Lord of the Church, speaking to these churches, urge them to tighten their ecclesiastical bonds to each other as a divine priority.

The Church of Ephesus, having lost its first love for

Jesus Christ, is urged to repent (Revelation 2:4 ff.). And since ecumenical promise is on our agenda, what does the Spirit promise? "To him that overcometh will I give to eat of the tree of life, which is in the midst of the paradise of God" (2:7).

And the Church in Smyrna? Faced by suffering, imprisonment and tribulation for their faith, believers are exhorted to be "faithful unto death, and I will give thee a crown of life. . . . He that overcometh shall not be hurt of the second death" (2:10-11).

And the Church in Pergamos, which condoned false doctrine and fornication? Repent quickly! is the summons, lest Christ Himself should fight the offending ones "with the sword of my mouth" (2: 16 ff.). "To him that overcometh will I give to eat of the hidden manna, and will give him a white stone, and in the stone a new name written . . ." (2:17).

And the Church in Thyatira, whose seductive teaching led Christians to fornication and to eat what was sacrificed to idols? The offenders are threatened with destruction unless they repent (2:20 ff.).

And what of the Church in Sardis? Its works were tawdry, and the Spirit pleads with trespassers to repent (3:1 ff.). "He that overcometh . . . shall be clothed in white raiment . . . and I will . . . confess his name before my Father, and before his angels" (3:5).

And the Church in Philadelphia? It had kept Christ's Word, and He in turn promises to keep believers "from the hour of temptation, which shall come upon all the world . . ." (3:10 ff.). "Him that overcometh will I make a pillar of the temple of my God . . . and I will write upon him the name of my God and the name of the . . . New Jerusalem . . . and my new name" (3:12).

And the Laodicean Church? Lukewarm in works, its

confidence lay in its own resources (3:14 ff.). It was urged
to repent. "To him that overcometh will I grant to sit
with me in my throne, even as I overcame and am set down
with my Father in his throne" (3:21).

So the Risen Christ addressed the seven churches of Asia
Minor. The Spirit stressed the need to *overcome*—not simply
disunity as such, but sin and the Evil One, heresy and
immorality. In the priestly prayer Jesus prayed that the
disciples might be united with Him as He and the Father
are one. The theme reappears in this message to Thyatira,
the church of seductive teaching and practice: "He that
overcometh, and keepth my works unto the end, to him
will I give power over the nations . . . *even as I receive
from my Father*" (2:26-27). And the theme reappears in
the very last of the seven letters, in the message to the lukewarm Laodicean Church: "To him that overcometh will I
grant to sit with me in my throne, *even as I overcome, and
am set down with my Father in his throne*" (3:21).

In the midst of the messages to the seven churches, in
the warning to Thyatira, appears a declaration from the
Risen Christ touching *all the churches*—a word that focuses
on His reflection of the Father, and the believers' reflection
of their Redeemer: *"All the churches shall know that I am
he which seartheth the reins and the hearts"* (2:23 ff.).
How will the world know that the Father hath sent Him if
the churches are unexposed to the searching claim of the
Risen Christ? And what does the Spirit promise? "He that
overcometh, and keepeth my works . . . to him will I give
power over the nations . . . even as I received from my
Father. And I will give him the morning star" (2:26 ff.).

It is painfully true, of course, that these churches in Asia
Minor soon vanished from the surface of history, and that
today the seven cities in Turkey perpetuate but the barest
remnants of their ruin. But they thus disappeared not be-

cause they failed to achieve visible organic union, nor because they failed to project a political strategy to modify the Roman empire, but because of disobedience to the invisible Head of the Church.

"All the churches shall know that I am he which searcheth the reins and the hearts" (2:23). The risen and reigning Christ searches the seat of the intellect, the desires of the will, and the depths of the emotions. His passionate concern is not union of church with church, but the transparent rule of Christ in the Christian community everywhere. If the Book of Revelation opens on the Church age, its closing words allude to the end of that age: "Blessed are they that do his commandments, that they may have right to the tree of life, and may enter in through the gates into the city. For without are dogs, and sorcerers, and whoremongers, and murderers, and idolaters, and whosoever loveth and maketh a lie. I Jesus have sent mine angel to testify unto you these things in the churches. [It is noteworthy that the Spirit here speaks to the *churches* even in anticipation of the end of the age.] I am the root and the offspring of David, and the bright and morning star. And the Spirit and the bride say, Come. And let him that heareth say, Come. And let him that is athirst come. And whosoever will, let him take the water of life freely. For I testify unto every man that heareth the words of the prophecy of this book, If any man shall add unto these things, God shall add unto him the plagues that are written in this book: And if any man shall take away from the words of the book of this prophecy, God shall take away his part out of the book of life, and out of the holy city, and from the things which are written in this book. He which testifieth these things said, Surely I come quickly. Amen. Even so, come, Lord Jesus. The grace of our Lord Jesus Christ be with you all. Amen" (22:14-21). On that basis, and on that basis alone, dare we hope that ecumenical promise will coincide with the promises of God.

The driving force of the ecumenical movement is its conviction that Christianity will effectively impress the world once diverse ecclesiastical traditions are lost in one single visible manifestation. If we have now truly reached the ecumenical age, men would everywhere have an impression of the unity of Christendom—and this is not the case. It may even be questionable whether the ecumenical process thus far has in fact produced that wider belief in the realities of the Christian religion which its sponsors adduce as the rationale or justification of the movement.

Let me propose a simple test. How many persons have been constrained to believe that Jesus is the Christ, the Son of the living God, through the church mergers which the ecumenical movement regards as the essence of Christian unity? I have yet to find one such person. Either we are not in "the ecumenical age," or what is called the ecumenical age as we now know it no more efficaciously impresses the world than did the pre-ecumenical era.

In closing it must be acknowledged that the ecumenical movement is perhaps the most significant religious development in twentieth century Christianity. It is high time that Christian churches moved out of the stone age and beyond the cold war era into the era of warm pursuit and mutual cooperation. But the interests of Christian unity do not necessarily coincide with the ecumenical movement. The problems of modern ecumenism run fully as deep as its promise, and the Great Head of the Church alone can give full substance to its promise and give deliverance from its problems. The deepest need of the churches is not organizational merger but the gift of repentance, and their surest bonding element is in union with Christ and under Him in devotion to His revealed truths and commandments.